OUR
VISITED PLANET

To

Steve Baker

may you be blest as
you read

OUR VISITED PLANET

WILLIAM M. JUSTICE

WORD SERVICES
LINCOLN, NEBRASKA

TO:
the friends in the seen and unseen worlds
whose love and prayers and fervor of thought
have made this book possible

CONTENTS

OUR
VISITED PLANET

CHAPTER ONE

THE VISITOR FROM OUTER SPACE

"Earth Listens for Other Worlds" is the title of a story in *The New York Times* that relates how astronomers at Green Bank, West Virginia, have now turned the eighty-five-foot dish antenna of their radio telescope towards the two stars, Tau Ceti and Epsilon Eridani, in an attempt to pick up signals that any possible inhabitants there might be trying to send us. The report warns that the odds against receiving anything is over a million to one. Nevertheless, the account goes on to state that the two stars, some 8.7 light years away, have characteristics that make the existence of life there conceivable; and that the project represents the beginning of human efforts to determine conclusively whether we are alone in the universe.

The question whether someone from outer space is trying to get in touch with the earth carries an appealing fascination. One wonders what might be the effect upon the public mind if an authentic message were received from another star, or a visitor from some distant planet was reported to have landed in London, Buenos Aires, or New Delhi. Public interest would doubtless mount to a new all-time high. The radio and television would momentarily report his doings. All of us would listen avidly to such reports for any information made available. Speculation would run high; and the curious might even travel great distances to get a glimpse of him and hear him speak.

Certain questions would be uppermost in our minds concerning the unknown visitor. Where did he come from? How did he get here? What sort of a man is he? And what was his purpose in coming? It would be most exciting to meet such a person and hear him talk. But if he were like us (and he would have to be if we talked with him), he would be limited in his knowledge. He could tell us certain things we do not know: for instance, what the planet he came from was like; how he got here; and how long it took him to make the trip. He might even show us the inner workings of his space ship, and the type of energy it used, from which our own scientists might derive clews to construct a new gadget.

All such things would be interesting, and in a measure useful; but mankind's most important questions would still remain unanswered. The matters that touch us most deeply have little to do with factual information. Our most fundamental questions are philosophical and religious and deal with the nature of reality and with ultimate values: What about the being and nature of God? What is he like? Is the universe friendly? What lies out beyond death? What is the meaning of life? Where did we come from, why are we here, and where are we going? These are the great issues of human existence; and in all probability, our visitor could not speak upon them with any more assurance than we can.

But suppose this outer-space visitor were not a man from Mars but a divine Being who came to us with the know-how of the universe, who knew the nature of ultimate reality and whose words carried the majesty of eternal truth. Suppose our visitor were no mere man but God himself in human form? The ensuing excitement on the earth would be immeasurably accelerated. This time the traffic would be in the opposite direction. Instead of rushing to see and greet the newcomer, many would head the other way. The incarnation of a true and holy God could be a frightening and upsetting thing; and few persons would have the moral confidence to risk an encounter with Righteousness itself. Orson Welles' invasion from Mars scare would be tame compared with the pandemonium that would break out once mankind became aware that the Creator of the universe had visited his earth in person.

To be sure, such ideas as these are pure speculation. They are on the same level as the great mass of science fiction that engrosses the youth of today. Yet, if the claims of the Christian religion be true, this incredible thing has already happened. Our earth, on one occasion, has entertained a divine Guest. In fact, the point of the Christmas story—to use J.B. Phillips' striking phrase—is that we now live on "a visited planet." A more august person than George Washington has been around; and over the front porch of the world a sign can now read, "God Almighty slept here." For if we are to accept the claims of Christianity as truthworthy, the awesome truth is that the very feet of God have trod this planet and his authentic voice once spoke to men like ourselves.

From the first century onward, the basic affirmation of Christian preaching has been that at a specific point in human history the mind and will of the eternal God encounters us in the historically active will of Jesus Christ. The great claim is that the Source of all truth and beauty and purpose was once particularized in a human life. This central event of time is the bedrock reality that gave rise to the Christian religion. It is the truth that overflows every page of the New Testament and is structured in all the great creeds of Christendom.

In the awesome words of the Nicene Creed, the early church asserted that the human Jesus was "God of God, Light of Light, very God of very God, begotten not made . . . who for us men and our salvation came down from heaven and was made man." This ancient formulation of faith does not stand solitary, but represents the consensus of belief that binds the Christian world together today. As a demonstration of this fact the constitution of the World Council of Churches, representing approximately 250 Christian denominations in 90 countries of the world, carries the structural statement that the council is "a fellowship of churches which accept our Lord Jesus Christ as God and Saviour."

This truth has been central in all the ancient creeds from Nicaea to Chalcedon, embodied in later historic confessions of faith, sung in the Church's music, chanted in its liturgy, and preached from every Christian pulpit on earth. If the incarnation of God in Christ is not authentic history, then of all peoples of the earth Christians are most to be pitied. They have been victimized by their own belief, and for centuries the Christian Church has been based on mountains of ecclesiastical hypocrisy and piously repeated inanities. The thing once happened; or else the whole machinery and pageantry of the Christian religion is without foundation, and the worship of the church is merely an empty show.

The rumor of this incredible happening has been floating around for over 1900 years; but mankind has never taken it as seriously as it might. Familiarity has deadened the minds of many brought up in the Christian tradition to its true significance. If we did not have a record of this God-event, easily available in the most widely printed book on earth and often selling for less than a dollar, we might appreciate it more; just as Emerson suggested that we might appreciate the stars more if they only came out once in a thousand years.

Since our childhood we have absorbed the story by a process of spiritual osmosis. We have seen it enacted at Christmas in pageantry and music, in picture and ritual, in nursery rhymes and carols; and have heard it droned from a thousand pulpits until it has lost its startling originality and has become tame and unexciting. Yet the sublime wonder and importance of the thing remains. Browning's Pope, in *The Ring and the Book*, contemplating how God chose the wayside planet as "stage and scene" of his transcendent act, observes that beside *that* fact and in comparison with it "even the creation fades into a puny exercise of power."

Admittedly, the momentous claims of historic Christianity that the earth has experienced a cosmic breakthrough are not easy to accept. From the first century onward men have debated the issue. All sorts of views have been expressed as to the nature of the event and all sorts of doubts have been raised as to its reality. How did the notion arise that our earth once entertained a divine Visitor? Who started the report in the beginning?

When we attempt to get back to the historic core of things for the source of the belief, we find the record of the event in certain original writings that sprang out of the life of the primitive Christian community which we now call the New Testament. It is to these documents we must refer. We find the idea is based on three historical realities embodied in these early records:

(a) The unique impression which the personality of Jesus Christ made on the world of his day.

(b) The estimate which Jesus himself held concerning his own person and mission.

(c) His continuing influence on the religious community and the life of the world.

As a primary reason for the original belief that we now live on a visited planet, let us first consider the effects which the personality of Jesus Christ had upon the men who knew him in the beginning. It is not easy to grasp the import of Jesus' earthly ministry to the people of his day. The impression they had of him is probably quite unlike that which many people brought up in the Christian religion now carry. Certainly the crowds that gathered around Jesus during his public ministry would have derived a much more vital and realistic comprehension of his manhood than the conventional stereotyped image presented in many churches and currently held today as the gentle Jesus meek and mild. It is necessary for the average person brought up in Sunday School to push beyond his baby picture of Jesus and re-read the New Testament frankly and freshly as though for the first time, in order to come to grips with the human and dynamic figure of Christ presented in the gospels.

A person thus reading the gospel records of Jesus' life might get a number of impressions of his image, of which mildness and gentleness would be a part, but only a part. While there was certainly a tender aspect to Jesus' personality, a tenderness comparable only to that of a woman of the most exquisite character; yet, if the inspired

15

accounts are to be trusted, this would never have been the first impression the disciples would have had of him. Meek he was, and a great many other things besides—mysterious, many-sided, unpredictable, bold—but never mild or tame.

A man from Mars, reading the New Testament and meeting for the first time the strangely realistic figure of Jesus described there, would hardly derive the notion of what is now often meant by a human Christ. Instead, he would likely get the impression of a powerful individual of the highest mental faculties, faculties that were a bewilderment to the Jewish leaders who opposed his teaching; a strange and unpredictable character who was the object of intense and stubborn controversy; a social prophet of a range and power as to be often mistaken for one of his great Hebrew predecessors such as Jeremiah or Elijah; a moral teacher of the loftiest and purest ethical ideals; and a mysterious, many-sided individual whose enigmatic sayings often sounded like the strange utterances of a Being beyond man.

The gospels are full of occasions when the force of Jesus' personality was felt by the people about him. The first thing that seemed to have caught their attention was the strength and originality of his teaching. In the opening phases of his public ministry, it was widely recognized that he taught them as one having authority and not as the scribes. The range and grasp of Jesus' thought, and his penetrating insight into the nature of things, were so remarkable as to create surprise on every hand. On more than one occasion we are told that the crowds that gathered about him were "astonished" at his doctrine; and the impression he made upon them was so striking that they exclaimed, "What a word is this! We have heard strange things today!" (Lk. 5:26)

Still more spectacular were the acts of healing he did among them. Next to the account of his passion and crucifixion, the account of Jesus' works of mercy and power upon the bodies and minds of men occupy the greatest space in the four gospels and seemed to attract the largest following. With the exception of the twelve, it seems that a large part of his first disciples were people like Mary Magdalene, whom he had healed of some physical or psychic disorder. The impression Jesus made upon the people about him was frequently so forceful that the record states they "were amazed and questioned among themselves saying, What thing is this that even the unclean spirits obey him?" Following one of his notable acts of healing in a secluded village, the local citizenry begged him to leave them, "for they were taken with a great fear." (Lk. 8:37)

It is clear that the personality of Jesus was a riddle, not only to the general public, but also to the men of his inner circle. His closest disciples were often mystified by something he said or did and were afraid to ask him; and on one occasion were so shaken by some aspect of his personality that "they feared exceedingly and wondered." (Lk. 8:25) Even Pilate, the Roman Governor, was puzzled by the enigmatic silence of Jesus at his trial and asked him the question, "Whence art thou?" On receiving no reply, we are told Pilate "was the more afraid."

Even beyond the originality of his teaching, or the striking nature of his acts of healing, was this impression of his inner character. The men who encountered Jesus in the first century saw in him a character of such awe-inspiring stature and quality as to be explained only in terms of a divine Being. It is clearly evident that the impression he made upon those who knew him was that of an inwardly perfect life. This impression of his moral perfection is implicit on every page of the gospels and in all the recorded utterances of Jesus. Behind everything he says or does is the penetrating reality of his spiritual Lordship. Every act and utterance of his life bears the mark of his moral authority and excellence.

Perfection is so far removed from human mortals that, aside from Jesus, no one ever made the impression of perfection or ever attempted to claim it. Among all the other supreme personalities of history there has always been a conscious falling short of the moral ideal. Confucius, the most honored of all Chinese and the founder of their religion, is recorded as saying toward the close of his life, "In letters I am perhaps equal to other men; but the character of the perfect man, carrying out in his conduct what he professes, is what I have not yet attained to."

So far from perfection were the founders of all other religions, that Mohammed, the originator of Islam, is expressly commanded in the Koran to pray for pardon for his sins; Moses, the instrument of divine revelation to the Hebrews, is recorded in the Old Testament as being excluded from entry into the Promised Land because of his disobedience; and the great Saul of Tarsus, now regarded as the outstanding Christian of all times, spoke of himself as "the chief of sinners." Aside from the one solitary example of Jesus, perfection of character is a thing unknown among men.

In addition, there is this further fact that not only can no one be found who ever laid claim to the ideal life; but no one can be discovered who ever looked upon the thing as possible. Epictetus, the great Stoic philosopher, regarded the ideal life as impractical; and Cicero went so far as to say that no one ever suggested what a perfect man would be like. But in the case of Jesus, he not only rises to the level of the ideal but he compels us to admit that he does. In a world where no man, however noble, ever made the impression of moral perfection, or ever conceived perfection as a possibility, a Man lived who made people believe that he was living it before their eyes.

The question most often asked about Jesus by his contemporaries was that of the puzzled Pilate: "What manner of man is this? From whence did he come?" This riddle seemed to be so much in the forefront of the public mind in the closing days of his earthly existence, that Jesus himself raised the issue with the twelve by his memorable question at Caesarea Philippi: "Who do men say that I, the Son of Man, am?" The Apostle Peter seems to have given the consensus of the inner group, as well as the estimate of all who later came to know Jesus, in the great climactic answer which became the cornerstone of Christian belief in succeeding centuries: "Thou art the Christ, the Son of the living God." (Mt. 16:13-16)

A second reason for believing our earth has had a divine Visitor is Jesus' evident confidence in the centrality of his own person and mission. In an evaluation of a man's character, what the man thinks of himself is even more revealing than what others may think of him. If the impression Jesus made upon his contemporaries was so remarkable, what was Jesus' own estimate of himself? Once we raise this question, we are confronted with one of the most arresting facts of history.

Unlike other great religious leaders, Jesus made his own person central in his message and deliberately drew attention to himself as the object of men's worship. "The dying Buddha," writes Wilhelm Herrmann, in *The Communion of the Christian With God*, "puts his confidence in the truth of his teaching; but he leaves his disciples the admonition that they may forget him, but they are to keep his teaching and the way he has shown them. Plato says the like of Socrates. Now in the whole range of history there are no other figures, apart from Jesus, which so surprise us with originality of moral strength as do these two. But while these two hid themselves modestly behind the teaching for which they lived and died, Jesus knew no more sacred task than to point men to his own Person."

Perhaps the most sobering thing about the portrait of Jesus which strikes us out of the New Testament is this sublime consciousness of his own purity—a purity so inward and genuine that he did not need to feel ashamed of himself or to shrink from the gaze of God. There is nothing else like it in the experience of mankind. In the case of every man who is morally growing, the holier in character and the purer in heart he becomes the more acutely conscious is he of the presence of sin and his own inner failure. With Jesus it was otherwise. There is not the slightest trace in his words of the humility associated with the saints. He never displays remorse; never suggests he has fallen into sin. What other man could have looked straight into the face of a hostile crowd and thrown out the challenge "which one of you convinces me of sin?" and still give no impression of arrogance or self-righteousness?

"In the gospels," says Herrmann, "Jesus shows us the portrait of a man who is conscious that he himself is not inferior to the ideal for which he sacrifices himself. The fact that Jesus thought of himself as sinless stands out powerfully before us when we remember what he said and did at the Last Supper with his disciples. In the face of a death whose horror he keenly felt, he was able to say that this death he was about to die would take away the burden of guilt from the hearts of those who should remember him. So mighty within him was the consciousness of his own purity, that in that hour when the conscience of every man who is morally alive inexorably sums up his life, this man could conceive of his own moral strength and purity as that power which alone could conquer the sinner's inmost heart and free him from the deepest needs."

The fact that Jesus made himself central in his total message and fostered the idea of his own uniqueness is apparent not only in the numerous specific statements to that effect, but still more in the inescapable assumptions that underlie all he said or did. That he thought of himself as having a relationship to the Source of Being unparalleled among all the sons of men is evident on every page of the gospels. Here is a man who goes about talking as if he were God. What are we to make of it? If he were emotionally unstable, or seeking an honor for himself, we would look upon him as made of common clay, a deluded fanatic like many we have heard of. But the case of Jesus is just the opposite. His is no fevered imagination. Apparently he has no hidden designs to further, no personal ambitions to accomplish. He manifests a completely selfless spirit. His speech is notably temperate, objective, reasonable. He is neither conceited nor overbearing, but amazes us continually with his humility of heart. Yet, as Chesterton once observed, we hear this strolling carpenter saying calmly and almost carelessly, like one looking over his shoulder, "Before Abraham was I am."

If the record of the life of Christ is a mere human story, then indeed it is a strange story. When we treat it in this way, we run into all sorts of difficulties of interpretation. Things just do not make sense. For if there is any description of Jesus that stands out with the most convincing realism, it is precisely the description of the supernatural. There is something transcendent about his person and words that defies description, but which is amazingly convincing.

He seems to have lived habitually on the borderline of two worlds, the seen and the unseen, and to be as much at home in the one as the other. It is impossible to read the gospels without getting the impression of a man who had tapped some hidden source of knowledge; who had inside information about the way the universe is run. There is the quality of first-hand reporting in all Jesus' utterances—just as though one were looking with unobstructed vision through a window upon a hidden world and merely reporting back what he saw.

At the point where every other man would be hesitant and uncertain, Jesus spoke with a directness and assurance that startles us. His manner of speaking is full of references to unseen facts and realities beyond the reach of normal cognition. A child is brought to him and he casually remarks that the guardian angels of such little ones "do always behold the face of my Father in heaven." (Mt. 18:10) Or his disciples return from their mission of preaching and healing, rejoicing over a success in which even the demons were subject to them, and he answers as calmly and in as matter-of-fact a way as if he were telling the time of day: "I beheld Satan as lightning fall from heaven." (Lk. 10:18) Or, on another occasion, the Sadducees raise with him the question about the marital status of the seven-times-widowed woman—whose wife she would be in heaven—and Jesus informs them that they are ignorant both of the Scriptures and the power of God, for in the resurrection "they neither marry nor are given in marriage, but are as the angels of God." (Mk. 12:25)

How did he know these things? Where did he get his information? If we are to interpret such statements as being anything more than poetic nonsense (and certainly if they are to be worthy of the intelligence of Jesus they must carry some modicum of empirical meaning), what are we to make of the person who spoke them? What indeed does it let us in for!

Contrary to the popular notion of things, Jesus was not crucified for proclaiming a new code of ethics or for teaching the Golden Rule, but for something far more startling and incriminating. The gravamen of the charges brought against him by the Jewish leaders had to do with certain claims they had heard him make about himself and his authority that sounded like the extravagant utterances of a demented fanatic who claimed to be a brother of the North Star or the Pleiades, one whose sinister implications constituted unspeakable blasphemy and threatened the very existence of the national state.

If there is one indisputable fact in the gospel story that stands pre-eminent and unmistakable out of a mass of circumstances and events related there, it is that the thing which brought Jesus into mortal conflict with the religious authorities of his day and eventually brought about his death was his peremptory assumption of powers and prerogatives reserved only for the Divine. Let us consider two examples of this out of a considerable number that might be chosen. Both of the examples are reported by all the synoptics and are among the best attested portions of the gospel records.

The first is the case of Jesus' healing of the paralytic, in which the charge against him is that of sacrilege. The accusation which the orthodox religious leaders brought against Jesus was that he forgave sins—not sins against himself, just sins. When he said to the palsied man, "Son, thy sins are forgiven thee," (Mk. 2:9) the Pharisees and scribes became livid with rage at his blasphemy, and rightly so; for he was presuming to do that which was the prerogative of God only. We are so familiar with the story that its implications cease to startle us; but Jesus' contemporaries were quick to see that forgiving somebody else's sins, other than wrongs done to one's self, is an unspeakable horror and perversion.

We can better bring home the true analogy in this way: Suppose a friend tells me a group of ruffians broke into his home, set fire to the building, and escaped with a quantity of plunder and I should say, "I forgive them all." What would be his reaction? Would he not regard my assertion as an impertinence so fantastic as to border on insanity? Yet it was no less than this on the part of Jesus that stirred the antagonism of the orthodox Jewish leaders and fanned their wrath into a passion against him. How could a spiritually sensitive Jew, dedicated to absolute monotheism, be anything but outraged by the action of Jesus in assuming the power of forgiving sins, a power that had never been conceded even to the Messiah.

The second illustration is that of the account of Jesus' trial before the Jewish Sanhedrin. Here the charges brought against him were those of sorcery and sedition. Witnesses were produced who testified they had heard Jesus make fantastic boasts of magical powers, saying he was able to destroy the Jewish temple and raise it up again in three days. A few hours later, when brought before Pilate, the Roman Governor, a further charge of treason was brought against him by the Jewish leaders who claimed Jesus had refused to pay tribute to Caesar, "saying that he himself is Christ, a king."

What colossal egotism could make a man, on trial for his life before a Jewish tribunal, seal his fate by an awesome assertion of Divinity—an assertion that threw the court into an uproar and caused its presiding officer to rend his garments and cry out against the blasphemy? As Frank

Morison points out in his valuable little book, *Who Moved the Stone?*, Jesus was condemned to death not by evidence produced by his accusers at his trial, but upon an admission exacted from him under oath, the solemn Oath of the Testimony, to which even silence itself was an unforgivable offense. All the synoptic writers record the fact that it was on Jesus' frank and unequivocal testimony against himself that the verdict of the court was rendered. The Gospel of Matthew relates the alternative presented to Jesus by Caiphas in words as definite and unmistakable as rocks:

And the high priest stood up and said, 'I adjure you by the living God, tell us if you are the Christ, the Son of God.' Jesus said to him, 'You have said so. But I tell you, hereafter you will see the Son of man seated at the right hand of Power, and coming on the clouds of heaven.' Then the high priest tore his robes, and said, 'He has uttered blasphemy. Why do we still need witnesses?' They answered, 'He deserves death.' (26:62-66)

What are we to make of this incident? As George Bernard Shaw suggests, if Jesus had been indicted in a modern court he would have been examined by doctors and on the strength of his testimony found to be obsessed by a delusion, declared incapable of pleading, and sent to an asylum. What explanation is there of his strange behavior? It is quite clear from the records that Jesus could have saved himself by merely remaining silent; yet under the circumstances he chose to speak. What reasonable objective, or even temporary advantage, did he hope to achieve by asserting such awesome powers as those he claimed? If Jesus' statement were not true, it could only represent the boastful rantings of a self-centered paranoiac who made the mistake of talking too much at the wrong time and place. But Jesus was hardly this. Yet under the circumstances, it would seem the only alternative left us is that Jesus was either the world's biggest simpleton, or else he was what he claimed to be.

Those who regard this central figure of history as merely an expression of man at his best, and whose unfailing rule of thumb is that "of two meanings always choose the less," must make what sense they can out of the gospel records. Personally, I have never been able to comprehend the mind that could accept the teachings of Jesus as inspired and authentic and deny the authenticity of the claims he made concerning his supernatural being. Anselm's dilemma, *aut deus, aut non bonus*, has always seemed to me to be incontrovertible. Jesus was either a divine being or else he was not even a good man.

The Messianic claims Jesus made are unprecedented in the history of mankind. There is a sort of notion in the air that there have been many persons throughout history who have laid claims to divinity. This is not true. Such claims are really so rare as to be unique. With the exception of Jesus, no one among the front ranks of men has ever thought of himself as divine. The most that any of the great ones ever claimed was that they were servants of the Divine.

Moses, the adored progenitor of the Jewish faith, did not claim divinity; nor did Confucius, revered above all Chinese. Aristotle, the father of logic and one of the keenest intellects who ever lived, never had the idea that he was the father of gods and men come down from the sky. It is indeed possible to find occasional individuals who have made crude and vainglorious claims of divinity; but we find them in precisely the places we would expect to find them—in lunatic asylums and padded cells, and not among the sages and founders of religion.

The greater a man is the less likely he is to make the highest claims. Socrates, the wisest man, knew he knew nothing; and Sir Isaac Newton, the great scientist, regarded himself as merely the picker-up of a few seashells of thought on the beaches of an infinite ocean. A great man knows he is not God; and the greater he is the better he knows it. Outside of the solitary case we are considering, nobody has ever seriously laid claims to divinity except charlatans and lunatics.

But nobody supposes that Jesus of Nazareth was that sort of person. He would be the last man in the world one might accuse of megalomania. In the Christ of the gospels there is a firmness of religious conviction, a breadth of intellect, and a purity and strength of will combined in no other figure in history. It would be impossible to class him with narrow-minded fanatics, crafty charlatans, or impostors. No one in his right mind has ever suggested that the author of the Beatitudes was a half-witted imbecile, or that the One who originated the Great Prayer was the sort of person who spent his time scrawling verses or drawing stars on the walls of a cell. By any possible measure of comparison he must be placed on a higher scale than that. Yet, by all human analogies, we have really to put him there, or else in the highest place of all.

In addition to the impression Jesus made upon the men of his day, and the estimate he had of himself, a final reason for believing we live on a visited planet is the fact of Jesus' continuing moral influence upon the life of the world. His effect upon Western civilization and the religious community that bears his name is so titanic as to warrant a belief in the supernatural quality of his being. Just as the size of a mountain dislodged into the sea by an earthquake may be judged by the tidal wave that follows, the spiritual stature of Jesus can be measured by the dislocation of events produced by his life. The magnitude of his influence upon the world has been given classic expression in a well-known sentence by Jean-Paul Richter to the effect that the history of Jesus of Nazareth has to do with him "who being the holiest among the mighty and the mightiest among the holy, with his nail-pierced hands lifted empires off their hinges and turned the stream of the centuries out of their channel."

If Jesus suffered delusions of grandeur about himself, he has not been alone in his fantasy, for a sizeable number of his contemporaries came to share them with him. Also an ever-widening circle of thoughtful minds in the centuries following have accepted his claims as authentic. It is reported that an American missionary, in presenting his Christian testimony to a Brahmin priest, asked him the question, "Could you say, as Jesus did, 'I am the resurrection and the life?' " The priest, in keeping with the Hindu conception of the divinity of all life, said, "Yes, I could say that." "But," replied the missionary, "could you get anybody to believe you?" This is the crux of the matter. In the case of Jesus, he not only made extravagant and unprecedented claims about his own person and mission, but he got a multitudinous host of others to believe them also.

The full significance of the fact that Jesus' first appeal was to members of a rigorously monotheistic race is often lost on us today. A Jewish friend's facetious remark to the effect that no Jew would ever think another Jew divine was intended as a humorous statement to be chuckled over; but it succinctly expresses the actuality of the matter. The men who started the rumor of a more than earthly Christ were an unlikely bunch of men to invent the dogma. As we have already noticed, they were devout Jews in whom monotheism was a passion and the ascription of divine honors to any but the supreme God a horror and a blasphemy. So deep was their prejudice against the act of deifying the mere human, that Philo, a liberal Jew and contemporary of Jesus, risked his life at the court of Caligula to protest against Jews being compelled to offer a few grains of incense in tribute to the genius of the Emperor. Yet these men who knew Jesus intimately did not hesitate to ascribe divine honors to him.

The belief of the persons who in the beginning were closest to Jesus became the living faith of the Church; and gave rise to that spectacular outburst of writings that later became the New Testament. The men who wrote these ancient documents were unanimous in their affirmation of the exalted uniqueness of Jesus; and spoke of him as the Divine Idea, the Word from beyond time. A few years after the death of Christ, the little Christian community had begun to look upon the world itself as the broad base of the altar on which he had been sacrificed; and within the lifetime of one man, the faith of the entire Church was summed up in that matchless sentence, "For God so loved the world that he gave his only begotten Son that whosoever believeth in him should not perish but have everlasting life."

Oddly enough, the first heresy of Christianity was not a denial of the deity of Christ but of his humanity. One would imagine first-century heretics would have questioned the former, rather than the latter; but such was not the case. The early Docetists all asserted Christ's divinity; but they denied he was a real man, saying that he only *seemed* to have suffered and died and to possess a fleshly body.

Aside from conscious fraud on the part of Jesus, the alternatives to accepting Jesus' estimate of himself as recorded in the Scriptural narratives are three:

(a) He was wholly misreported.

(b) He was mentally unbalanced.

(c) He was hopelessly mistaken.

Unless one is ready to give up the portrait of Jesus found in the New Testament as entirely untrustworthy, the first of these three alternatives cannot be successfully maintained. The argument that the written records of his life have been wholly misreported or invented, and that the strangely moving Figure they bear witness to is completely false, is a proposition no competent scholar would undertake to maintain. On the other hand, there is a self-authenticating quality about the portrait of Jesus in the New Testament that commands belief; which no amount of "de-mythologizing" can obliterate.

How does it come about that the gospels, fragmentary as they admittedly are, can combine to portray a human image so consistent in character, so sublime in moral qualities, and so impressively real as the figure of Jesus Christ that we meet in the pages of the New Testament? Even though it may be easily demonstrated that the gospels came from a number of sources, that they contain many strata of documents, and were possibly not written by the four authors whose names they bear but pseudonymously and by later hands; it simply confounds the mystery. For the more complex the origin of the records, the greater is the marvel of the resultant portrait they present. The personality of Jesus is something that could never have happened; and yet it could not have been invented. The story itself is inconceivable; yet the invention of it would have been a miracle as solitary as the creation.

The reality of Jesus' belief in his supernatural being is so implicit in all he said and did that to deny the fact is to make nonsense out of the whole gospel story. Such facts and statements as we have been considering are so much a structural part of the inspired records, so germane to the total message of historic Christianity, that to eliminate or disregard them as unhistorical is to make a travesty of the entire New Testament, and to deny any valid reason for believing Jesus ever existed as an actual person.

In this event we would be brought to the unreasonable position of maintaining that all traces of the earthly life of the man who had had the greatest influence in history have disappeared. The absurdity of this course is suggested by Dr. T.R. Glover, late Professor of Ancient History at Cambridge University, when he said, "If the ordinary canons of history hold good, Jesus is undoubtedly an historical person. If he is not an historical person, the only alternative is that there is no such thing as history at all—it is delirium, nothing else; and a rational being would be better employed in the collection of snuff-boxes. And if history is impossible, so is all other knowledge."

As to the second alternative, that Jesus was mentally unbalanced and suffered delusions of grandeur, it is sufficient to point out that twenty centuries of Christian history were doubtless not created as a monument to a megalomaniac. Such mighty results as have followed his teaching and example do not flow from so questionable a source. The influence of this Man has been without parallel in all the annals of the race. The French critic Renan speaks of Jesus as "the incomparable Man, to whom the universal conscience has decreed the title of the Son of God, and that with justice." Just as there are certain absolutes in nature, such as the speed of light and the quality of sound, the personality of Jesus rises above us like a star, incandescent with spiritual ultimates. He has become the norm and archetype of humanity in whom the idea of the species is incarnate, and in whose person all that belongs to the perfection of every man is included. It is not likely that either the sanity or goodness of such a person can be successfully challenged. It is a little late in the day to cry either imbecile or fraud to the Figure on the cross.

If it is incredible that Jesus was wholly misreported, or mentally unbalanced, it is equally inconceivable that he was completely mistaken as to who he was. If it should turn out that he was mistaken at this point, he was not alone in his error. There were others who shared his delusion. If Jesus were merely a man, then he was a badly mixed-up man and his contemporaries who knew him best were likewise badly mixed-up. In addition to this, many of the loftiest and purest minds of succeeding centuries have been deluded as well, for they also have fallen under his sway and have acknowledged his claims. For almost two millenia men have not only called him Lord and Master, but God and Saviour.

As an example of this, witness the words of William Shakespeare, the universal Englishman and the world's greatest poet, whose last will and testament, now preserved in the British Museum, bears eloquent testimony to this fact. In this document, the man who wrote the gigantic masterpieces *Lear, Othello,* and *Macbeth* is on record as having said humbly and finally in his closing earthly request: "I commend my soul into the hands of God, my Creator, hoping and assuredly believing, through the only merits of Jesus Christ, my Saviour, to be made partaker of life everlasting." Shakespeare is merely one of untold millions who have come to the moment of death with the name of Jesus on their lips, and have entrusted themselves and their eternal destiny into his hands.

The riddle of the person of Christ remains the mystery of all time. What other man, however great or good, would have dared to say, "He that hath seen me hath seen the Father." Imagine a great world leader or statesman, such as the late Sir Winston Churchill, announcing one day in the morning news that if the public wanted to know what God is like, they could look at Her Majesty's Prime Minister and see for themselves. In this event, everybody would know that something far more serious than senility had struck the old warrior. Yet such an assertion would be no more extravagant than many Jesus made concerning himself.

With amazing confidence he says, "Heaven and earth shall pass away, but my words will not pass away." Pre-emptively, and almost with a wave of his hand, he sets aside a millennium of Jewish traditions and the magisterium Law of Moses by declaring, "It hath been said of old; but I say unto you . . ." He claims the awesome power to forgive sins. He places loyalty to himself above the most binding of earthly ties, including loyalty to home and family. He carries his claims to their extreme moral and ethical limits by setting himself up as judge of men on the last day, and making men's attitude toward him decisive in determining their ultimate destiny. He held that within his own person the purposes of God's creation were summed up. Was he mistaken? Was his belief in himself and the consciousness of his life mission only a delusion? The very thought of such a possibility has about it the chill of death, as though the sun itself had disintegrated and disappeared from the sky.

There are many questions in the world that have never been settled, but there is one fact that becomes more certain as the centuries roll on: namely, the absolute and pre-eminent moral authority of Jesus Christ. He looms over all the world as the one Universal Man who typifies humanity and is at home in all ages and lands and among all people. His memory, which has been preserved in written records and enshrined in the New Testament, is the greatest thing the race has. It is mankind's glimpse of a Figure of superhuman moral loveliness that emerged from the hidden depths of infinitude and walked the earth for a time, never to be forgotten. But Jesus Christ is more than memory. He is a substance that is still alive, a force to be reckoned with in the world today. What John Henry Newman wrote in the nineteenth century is even more true today:

There is just one Name in the world that lives; it is the Name of One who passed His years in obscurity, and who died a malefactor's death. Eighteen hundred years have gone by since that time, but still it has its hold upon the human mind. It has possessed the world and it maintains possession. Amid the most varied nations, under the most diversified circumstances, in the most cultivated, in the rudest races and intellects, in all classes of society, the Owner of that great Name reigns. High and low, rich and poor, acknowledge Him. Millions of souls are conversing with Him, are venturing at His word, are looking for His presence. Palaces sumptuous, innumerable, are raised in His honor; His image in its deepest humiliations, is triumphantly displayed in the proud city, in the open country, in the corners of streets, on the tops of mountains. It sanctifies the ancestral hall, the closet, and the bedchamber; it is the subject for the exercise of the highest genius in the imitative arts. It is worn next to the heart in life; it is held before the failing eyes in death. Here, then, is One who is not a mere name; He is no empty fiction; He is a substance; He is dead and gone, but still He lives—as the living, energetic thought of successive generations, and as the awful motive power of a thousand great events.

It was this supreme Personality, who once climbed the hills and walked the dusty roads of the Middle East, who gave to mankind the unforgettable impression that we now live on a visited planet.

CHAPTER TWO

THE MAN OF DEATH

When a man reads the New Testament as a whole, without spectacles of one kind or another but with a fresh, open-minded approach as though reading it for the first time, he can hardly fail to be struck by certain great insights. Three sovereign ideas will stand out as prominently as the face of the Matterhorn:

(a) Jesus Christ came into the world on a cosmic mission, effecting a deliverance for all men beyond their own power to achieve.

(b) The death of Christ was not a martyrdom but a self-offering, something which he of his own volition accepted as the inevitable necessity of the divine mission he had come to fulfill.

(c) His death has done something to eternally change for the better the human situation on this planet.

As we have already noted, the central fact of the Christian religion is the Incarnation. Men may accept or deny it; but the truth stands solitary in human history as the sublime affirmation of the Christian gospel. The early Christian documents throb with a sense of the enormity of a great reconciling process undertaken by a supreme Personality who, from the heights of timeless being, entered into human existence to accomplish something for mankind that could not have been accomplished otherwise.

It is this transcendental element in the apostolic belief against which the modern mind most strenuously reacts. Yet it was Jesus himself who furnished evidence for the belief in his pre-incarnate life—that prior to his coming into the world he had known an unending existence in the being of God of which his earthly life formed only a momentous episode. The contradiction between the power and sanity of his moral teaching and the colossal megalomania that must lie behind his theological teaching concerning himself, unless he is what he claimed to be, has never been successfully surmounted.

The de-mythologizers can de-mythologize as they may; but the fact that the early Christians believed in the deity and pre-existence of Christ, and believed that he himself believed it, is as certain as any truth in the New Testament. Behind all the facts and explanation of facts dealing with the earthly life of Jesus is the momentous assumption of a divine Being whose existence antedated the world. The idea saturates the entire Fourth Gospel. It is the major argument of the Epistle to the Hebrews. It dominates the writings of St. Paul. It is implicitly structured in each of the synoptic gospels and constitutes the broad context of the whole apostolic message.

The thing which gives the doctrine its most striking quality is that it is not usually specifically asserted so much as it is taken for granted as the major pre-supposition from which all lesser doctrines are derived. The Apostle Paul, in taking a collection for the poor saints in Jerusalem, urges his fellow Christians to greater generosity in giving in order that they may follow the example of the Lord Jesus "who, though he was rich, yet for your sakes he became poor; that ye through his poverty might be rich." (II Cor. 8:9) And on another occasion, when two women of his church at Philippi were at odds with each other, he admonishes them to have within themselves the mind of compassion and sacrifice which was in Christ Jesus, "who being in the form of God, thought it not robbery to be equal with God; but made himself of no reputation, and took upon him the form of a servant, and was made in the likeness of men." (Phil. 2:6)

However distasteful it may be for rationalistic thought to accept the concept of pre-existence, in the case of Jesus there does not seem to be any escape from it. The narratives that describe him give the unmistakable impression of a Being beyond time who moved and breathed in the sphere of an unlimited chronology. The final act of intercession in the closing hours of his Passion is one of many examples of this unparalleled self-consciousness of Jesus. In the great High Priestly Prayer recorded in the seventeenth chapter of the Gospel of John, we are permitted an intimate glimpse into the inner consciousness of Jesus. Here, in what has been called "the holiest spot in the New Testament," we are made to realize his lonely eminence in the moral and spiritual world.

It is not possible for us to follow the ascending course of an unstained soul as it rises to the consummation of divine communion; but as we listen to his words, we realize that we are standing by the high altar of the world. As the self-disclosure deepens in intimacy, it deepens in mystery. We feel that this Man carries humanity and all the ages on his heart. What is he saying? "Father, glorify thou me with thine own self; with the glory which I had with thee before the world was." If language means anything, here is a man in the highest and most supreme moment of his self-disclosure solemnly avowing the fact that in the unscalable heights of pre-creation days he was conscious of having known a luminous existence in the unbeginning life of God. It is well that we try to understand all we can of the self-consciousness of Jesus; but we ought to know when he is beyond us. The mind that could frame such a sentence can only leave us wondering.

The New Testament is abundantly clear that the significance of Jesus' earthly ministry derived its meaning from vast and transcendent antecedents. One never understands the Christian gospel unless it is seen in the light of an eternal background. The thing that gave the primitive message its moving appeal was that the story dealt with the drama of a divine Personality who descended from the heights of absolute being into time and space, only to re-ascend again carrying with him mankind's supreme destiny, much as a diver might descend to the dark and chilly depths of ocean and return with a priceless pearl in his possession. In the language of Christian thought this has been called the Kenosis, or the Divine self-emptying. The unmistakable implication is that God took action within the human life of Jesus in order that he might henceforth take action within all human lives. The mission was epitomized in those wistful words, "God sent not his Son into the world to condemn the world; but that the world through him might be saved." (John 3:17)

The second great insight of the New Testament is that the creative center and point of reference for this vast cosmic movement of human redemption was the death of Christ. In order to grasp the full significance of the truth, it is necessary to bear in mind that Jesus' earthly career was a genuinely empirical thing. While Christianity is unmistakable in its witness to the divine nature of Christ, it holds with equal insistence to his complete humanity. Jesus was a real man, not a demigod; and certainly not God playing man. His human nature was no disguise to be assumed and thrown off later like a discarded garment. The choices and decisions that confronted him during his earthly existence were real ones, not chimeras. The final outcome of his life mission was no foregone conclusion guaranteed by divine fiat. Conceivably it could have failed. Jesus became truly man; and since man is more than a body, this does not mean merely the physical part of man. He became man in personality and spirit as well as body. Since limitation is a characteristic of humanity, this involved limitation.

The great assertion of the Christian religion is that he who came into the world to save sinners was genuinely and authentically one of us. No one-sided biblicism must ever be allowed to obscure this fact. A singular point of difference, however, is seen in the end design of Jesus' mission. Unlike other great figures of history who seemed to have been born for the purpose of living and accomplishing some particular task in the world, Jesus is unique in that he seemed to have been born for the purpose of dying. For other men death

would have been an accident, an upset to their careers; but
for him, it seemed to be the fulfillment of his life goal, the
one definite thing he came into the world to do. The
evidence for this viewpoint is so overwhelming in the gospels
that it is impossible to escape the sacrificial view.

Jesus was pre-eminently a Man of Death. A sinister
shadow hung over his entire career. At his birth there was a
price on his head and he was listed in the "wanted" column.
He grew up among fierce nationalistic conflicts and under the
shadow of a sharp and pitiless sword. Since crucifixion was
the ordinary method of execution by the Romans, it is
practically certain that from his earliest years Jesus witnessed
numerous examples of man's inhumanity to man. The Jewish
historian Josephus, who was a contemporary of Jesus, in his
Wars of the Jews tells of an incident that happened in the
year 6 A.D. Jesus was at this time ten years of age, and so it
must have had an unforgettable effect upon the growing boy.

A Galilean named Judas gathered together a company of
rebels and attacked and captured the city of Sepphoris near
Nazareth. The Romans, with their usual ruthless efficiency
following a protracted siege, captured the city and burned it
and crucified two thousand of the rebels on the hill upon
which the city was built. From the rim of the mountains on
which Nazareth rests, one can look across a narrow valley to
Sepphoris some two or three miles away and clearly see all
that goes on there. The appalling impression of a burning city
under siege and the gruesome sight of a hillside covered with
crosses must have made an indelible impression on the
sensitive mind of Jesus.

The problem of securing wood for two thousand crosses in
a country as barren of timber as that of Galilee is no small
matter; and since Jesus' earthly father, Joseph, was a
carpenter, might it not have been possible that a Roman
officer commandeered Joseph and other carpenters of the
neighborhood to build these crosses? Did the boy Jesus
perchance wander over to the outskirts of Sepphoris to talk
with dying men on crosses, or to give some poor wretch a

drink of water to quench his thirst? We shall never know. But one thing is certain. Long before his own execution, Jesus must have known from first-hand observation the nature of crucifixions; and this knowledge gave content to his own strange and intuitive premonition that he himself was ultimately destined to hang upon a cross.

The background of Jesus' life was notably full of public acts of violence. He begins his ministry at a time of brutal murders, including the violent deaths of two false Messiahs (Luke 13:1; Acts 5:36). On his return to Nazareth following his baptism, his own townsmen attempt to assassinate him by casting him headlong from the brow of a cliff. He was passionately hated by the orthodox religious leaders of his day. The author of the Fourth Gospel mentions twenty-six instances of their intention to destroy him. As he moved toward the culmination of his public ministry, the certainty of his rejection and death at the hands of men became more definite and unmistakable.

In the closing days of the Passion, as Jesus was going up to Jerusalem for the final confrontation with his enemies, there was something so strange and unaccountable in his bearing that Mark tells us the disciples "were amazed and as they followed him they were afraid." Three times—like the solemn tones of a muffled bell—he warns them, "The Son of Man must go unto Jerusalem and suffer many things of the elders and chief priests and scribes and be killed." This thrice-repeated prediction—which Wellhausen thought as solemn and sacred as the story of the Passion itself—was the knell of a King about to die. The story of Christ is the story of a journey whose goal is death.

The conventional notion of Jesus' career is that it was the collapse of idealism, the upset of a good man's dream. It is said, somewhat with a sigh, "How unfortunate that the poor fellow was defeated by his enemies and the splendid purpose of his life shattered when it might have been such a success!" This is anything but the true picture. There is evidence to support the view that the cross was not an upset but the mechanism of a master strategy. It had design and intention about it. To regard Jesus simply as a victim of the blindness and cruelty of men is to miss the gospel point. "If you pity Christ," someone warned, "you are not seeing him." Jesus was not a simpleton, outwitted by evil men and destroyed. He knew what he was doing, he chose his course, and never once did he deviate from it. No man ever hesitated less. Calvary seemed to be in the forefront of his vision early in the game; and with unfaltering devotion, almost with military precision, he moved steadily toward the great act of sacrifice to which the will of God impelled him.

To interpret properly the significance of Jesus' career, it is necessary to view it in the light of a transcendent goal that had far-reaching but genuinely human and political implications. We cannot know what takes place in the holy of holies of any man's soul—much less in the pure and dedicated soul of Jesus—but the glimpse we are given in the New Testament of the inner consciousness of Jesus suggests that the supreme choice of his earthly career was consummated in a final act of his will so gigantic that our own wills cower before it. We are made to see that his life was controlled by thoughts and anticipations so vast and lofty that our own minds cannot rise to them.

A great Jewish judge of the Supreme Court once remarked to Norman Thomas, "One of the ironies of history is that the most militaristic and acquisitive nations of history should have chosen a pacifist Jewish peasant, not only as their prophet, but as their God." But history records an even greater irony; namely, that while Jesus was one of the most ambitious men that ever walked the earth—one who had vaster and more far-reaching plans of human conquest than any other—men continue to think of him in terms of humility. A colossal egotist like Rameses II in ancient Egypt, or a paranoid Hitler in the present century, never made such extensive claims for themselves, and neither did they aspire to such dizzying heights of power as did Jesus. Yet the sober judgment of mankind asserts that Jesus aspired to no crown that was not rightfully his, and throughout the centuries men continue to speak of him as the meek and lowly Nazarene.

Among earth's Caesars none had more ambitious plans or carried a greater consciousness of power than did Jesus. From the day Jesus walked out of Joseph's carpentry shop for his rendezvous with John the Baptist on the River Jordan, he was possessed of the loftiest dream that ever animated a human breast—the dream of the Kingdom of God. Alexander the Great is reputed to have sat down on the seashore after he had finished his conquests and wept because there were no more worlds to conquer. But the goal of this Man was something more than earthly. He thought in terms of a timeless kingdom and of universal and eternal rule.

Sir Winston Churchill is quoted as saying just prior to his death, "The Empires of the future are the Empires of the mind." It was the invisible empire of the mind that Jesus chose as his field of conquest. Other public leaders of his day thought purely in terms of political rule; he thought in terms of spiritual purpose. The end he sought was not political control but a revolution in the innermost places of the human spirit. Unifying and administering the affairs of a great world-state, difficult as this might have been, would have been child's play compared to the choice which Jesus eventually made. His ultimate objective was not the coercion of extensive geographical areas into obedience to law; rather, it was the stupenduous operation of transforming the thoughts and wills of men and thus altering the spiritual climate of moral continents. It was this massive undertaking to which Jesus committed himself.

The account of this epochal choice at the beginning of his public career is embodied in that priceless story of the Temptation, which must have come from Jesus himself, since he is the only one who could have told it. Following the great illumination at his baptism by the hands of John the Baptist at the River Jordan, when the consciousness of his divine being and mission blossomed into complete certainty as heaven opened in the deep of his soul and he heard the Great

Voice saying, "Thou art my Son, my Beloved!" Jesus was led by the Spirit—Mark says "Driven by the Spirit"—into the wilderness for a prolonged period of mental struggle and prayer. In the description of this momentous period of meditation, we are given in symbolic form a resume of the main elements of the travail of Jesus' soul as he stood on the threshold of his public ministry and decided his goals and strategies in the light of the will of God. Here he faced the alternatives of his life work and formulated the ultimate goal from which he never later deviated. Three things are clearly brought out in the story:

(a) The idea of political rule was in the mind of Jesus early in the game and represented an optional choice in his life mission.

(b) This course of action must have made a definite appeal to him, for otherwise it would have been no genuine temptation.

(c) But Jesus rejected the idea of a political Messiahship as incompatible with the will of God and chose another way.

The thought of political rule for an expected Messiah was ever present in the minds of Jesus' countrymen. An underground movement was in existence during his day; and a number of nationalistic organizations were dedicated to the task of throwing off the yoke of Rome and setting up an independent Jewish kingdom. In fact, one of Jesus' disciples was a member of a fanatical Jewish sect called Zealots, which bitterly opposed the Roman domination of Palestine. On one occasion, judging from a detail of history preserved in the Fourth Gospel, there was an actual movement afoot to seize Jesus and make him "King," that is to say the figurehead of a revolutionary movement against Rome, but we are told he hid himself alone in the mountains to avoid it. The independent kingdom established by the Maccabees was in the memory of every loyal Jew; and was a continual reminder that, however hopeless the outward appearance might be, the odds were not too heavy for a person of dedicated will such as Judas Maccabeus had been.

The common view is to regard Jesus as a first-century figure that could have cut no ice, or made any impression on the power politics of his day. But this is to ignore the historical circumstances of the times in which he lived and to underestimate the potential strength of a personality like his. We hesitate to speak thus of Jesus because he was so much more; but if political leaders of the first century were comparable to those of the present, then from a mere human standpoint alone, there were doubtless many who attained the highest positions in government with vastly less originality and fewer personable qualities than he. Gunnar Myrdal, the famous Swedish economist and social historian, quotes an outstanding Swedish diplomat as saying to his son, "My son, my son, if you only knew with what little wisdom the world is ruled."

That world rule was a possibility for a man like Jesus does not seem so remote when we consider the case of the Roman Emperor Vespasian, whose reign took place some forty years after the crucifixion. Vespasian was a common soldier who served with the Roman legionnaires in Germany and, by his own efforts, rose from the ranks to become commander of the legion. On the death of Otho in 69 A.D. the throne was left in doubt. So popular had Vespasian become that the soldiers of his own legion proclaimed him Emperor of Rome; he then ascended to the throne of the known world. It is not fantastic to assume that with Jesus' unique mental and spiritual endowment, his profound insight into human character, and his ability to inspire loyalty in others, had he been willing to compromise with the methods of the world he would have been something more than a second Judas Maccabeus and could have held in his hands the awesome power of empire.

If political control were a realistic option with Christ why did he not take it? It seems he did seriously consider the idea for a time before eventually rejecting it. His final temptation carried the hard-core offer of "all the kingdoms of the world and the glory of them." It was this glittering prospect that enthralled him during his grim sojourn in the desert. There is little doubt that Jesus thought of himself in terms of a certain kind of kingship and that political rule had a particular fascination for him. No one can be tempted by that which he does not want; and since a person is most strongly tempted at the point of his greatest power, there are reasons to believe that of the three temptations which confronted him as possible strategies of his future mission, the third was the most subtle and commanding.

To a person of Jesus' spiritual makeup, a base and sordid evil would have had no appeal. The choice must represent a high level of alternatives in order for either to be attractive to him. For this reason, we should look upon the issue which confronted Jesus at the opening of his ministry not as a clear-cut choice between good and evil; but rather as a choice between two courses of action, each of which held a promise for good, but only one of which represented the supreme good. Had the lesser of the two objectives been chosen, the world would still have greatly benefitted by the choice. Since capable leaders of government have long been in short supply, who would deny that a dynamic and humanitarian world leader such as Jesus would have been an enormous blessing to mankind.

A benevolent ruler who even approximated the spiritual and mental stature of Jesus would, as head of a world confederacy, have an influence for good in human affairs far beyond all calculation. A dedicated international statesman such as the late Dag Hammarskjold, Secretary General of the United Nations, located at a strategic point of power can lift the world to new levels of vision and cooperation. How much more would this have been true of Jesus, had he chosen to be a new type of Caesar.

Thus we see that the career of Christ is the story of one who might have been king but was not—of a man who could have reigned and who for a time wanted to reign, but who refused to reign. If Jesus could have had kingship on his own terms, unquestionably he would have accepted it as the supreme consummation of his earthly ministry. For a brief moment, he seems to have felt that the two incompatibles, the political and the spiritual, might be joined. But his penetrating realism led him to the undeniable fact that a spiritual Messiahship could not be implemented apart from the political; and that this meant a clash with the Roman garrison at Jerusalem, a revolutionary uprising of the Jewish people, certain conflict with the military power of Rome, and war and bloodshed on a vast scale. This would be a contradiction of his whole spirit and mission.

So consciously, deliberately, and with full knowledge of the issues involved, he set it aside and chose another way. An echo of this momentous choice was later heard at his inquisition before the Roman Governor. When Pontius Pilate demanded of Jesus to tell him plainly if he were the king of the Jews, with particular incisiveness Jesus replied, "If my kingdom were of this world, then would my servants fight." (John 18:36)

Chesterton says that there is something defiant about Christmas that makes the abrupt bells at midnight sound like the great guns of a battle that has just been won. This imagery is most apt. If it was at Bethlehem, the scene of the great Christmas Event, where the celestial war for human redemption potentially had its beginning, it was on the Mount of Temptation that the opening guns of the campaign were first heard and the advance started. From the standpoint of divine strategy, the human temptation of Jesus was the opening assault against the gates of hell.

Conscious of mysterious promptings and hitherto undreamed of powers within himself, Jesus faced the dreadful alternatives of his life mission. From the top of the high mountain, he sees all the kingdoms of the world in a moment of time. He feels the shuddering whisper of the Tempter: "All these things I will give you if you fall down and worship me." In the soul of him in whom the hopes and fears of the race are concentrated, for a brief time there oscillated those awesome possibilities. The infinite scales were momentarily poised while destiny hung in the balance; but with majestic decision came the unequivocal response: "Hence, Satan, thou shalt worship the Lord thy God and him only shalt thou serve." Right then he voted for Calvary. Following this gigantic and incomprehensible struggle, the Prince of the Universe came forth exhausted but triumphant. He then moved to the fulfillment of his divine mission in the singular peace of one who had thought out all his plans, and from thereon there would be no upsets or surprises.

In the final days before his crucifixion, Jesus seems to be moving and acting in the presence of the ages. There is a sublime grandeur about his person and an awesome sense of destiny in his bearing. His eyes seem to be looking far beyond the immediate present; and there is a final concentration of all his energies in what would appear to be the consummation of a deliberate and far-reaching purpose. He appeared to feel that the laying down of his life would be the potential realization for all men of eternal life in God; and in the act of giving himself in this way, the whole center of gravity of the moral universe would be shifted forever. None of his contemporaries could understand it at the time; but if the record of Jesus' words is to be trusted, he knew he was doing just that.

In spite of the opposition and the connivings of his enemies in Jerusalem, he ascends to the mounting climax of his life-dream with the masterly sureness of one who has himself planned it, foreseen it, and had chosen his part. Always Jesus gives us the impression of holding back vast reserves of power. He is not the hunted fugitive seeking to avoid capture. Instead, he goes to a secret rendezvous and waits patiently for his enemies to come and take him. In Pilate's judgment hall he is the master, not the prisoner. That awesome silence before his accusers is the supreme expression of spiritual power. Even on the cross, he has ascended above the reach of his enemies and has attained a position of such spiritual superiority as to be occupied in his closing breath in praying for his enemies. This is physical and spiritual mastery of a degree never seen in the world before or since.

Jesus repudiated the narrow nationalistic and political ambitions of his people and the use of military force to attain the ends of God—ends which today we refer to as "fighting for freedom," "preventing aggression," "establishing liberty and justice," and by other euphemistic terms. In doing this, he was breaking away from the conventional line of action taken by all other would-be saviours and was using an entirely new strategy. If he had been as stupid as Machiavelli or the Pentagon in trying to accomplish his end, he would have used the same kind of weapons as they recommend, with the same short-lived, disastrous results. But he was too original to follow the stale and questionable methods of military force, for he knew as none other ever did how the means determine the end; that peace does not blossom from the battlefield, that goodwill does not spring out of hatred, and that it is not easy for those who take the sword to relinquish it. The sword or the cross were the alternatives that faced him at the beginning of his career; and he chose the latter to the everlasting benefit of mankind.

The strategy of the cross that Jesus employed represents the ultimate wisdom of life, but mankind has been slow to learn it. The conventional notion is to discount the effect of spiritual forces and to regard military power as the ultimate power. It was this limited and short-ranged viewpoint that prompted Stalin, when someone mentioned in his presence the power of the Pope, to blandly ask, "How many divisions has he?" It was a similar blind arrogance to which Woodrow Wilson gave expression in castigating those who disagreed with his war policy in 1917. Said Mr. Wilson: "What I am opposed to is not the feeling of the pacifists but their stupidity. My heart is with them, but my mind has a contempt for them. I want peace, but I know how to get it, and they do not."

But did Mr. Wilson know how to get peace? History has something pretty definite to say at this point. The military method did not succeed. The war "to end war and make the world safe for democracy" did not either end war or make the world safe for democracy. What with stockpiles of hydrogen bombs growing, guided missiles flying about us, and the security of everybody decreasing as military buildups increase, even the "big power" boys are beginning to wonder if there might not be more to Jesus' way than there appears to be on the surface.

Contemporary history is a running commentary on the soundness of Jesus' technique of redemption and the ultimate strength of truth and love. Dr. Arnold Toynbee, whose monumental studies of world civilizations have caused him to be spoken of as the greatest historian since Thucydides, analyzes the twenty-three great civilizations that have risen and fallen since the dawn of time and finds that with practically no exception militarism was the root of their downfall. After discussing in *The Study of History* the several types of saviours and benefactors from ancient times, men of creative genius who sought the renewal of human society, he sums up his survey with the verdict that the Saviour with the Sword does not save. He says:

When we set out on this quest we found ourselves moving in the midst of a mighty host, but, as we pressed forward, the marchers, company by company, have fallen out of the race. The first to fail were the swordmen, the next the archaists and futurists, the next the philosophers, until only gods were left in the running. At the final ordeal of death, few, even of those would-be saviour gods, have dared to put their title to the test by plunging into the icy river. And now, as we stand and gaze with our eyes fixed upon the farther shore, a single figure rises from the flood and straightway fills the whole horizon. There is the Saviour; "and the pleasure of the Lord shall prosper in his hand; he shall see the travail of his soul and shall be satisfied."

A third great structural insight in the New Testament is

that the death of Christ has made a lasting and qualitative difference to human existence on the earth. Christianity is solitary among all the great religions of the world in that its worship is focused upon the death of its Founder. No other religion of ancient or modern times has ever had a cross at its center. In one of his great descriptive passages dealing with the uniqueness of Christianity, the nineteenth-century Jewish writer, Heinrich Heine, relates a scene from Homer's *Illiad* in which all the Greek gods are pictured as gathered on Mount Olympus in a great banquet. He describes how they feasted all day until the setting sun. Wine was poured from left to right and laughter unquenchable arose amid the blessed gods. Apollo played his beautiful lyre and the Muses sang alternately with sweet voices. Suddenly, amid this scene of revelry and feasting, a pale blood-stained Jew burst in upon them, wearing a crown of thorns on his head and bearing upon his shoulders a huge cross. He hurled the cross on the great banquet table till all the goblets shook; and all the gods were stricken dumb, and grew pale and ever paler till they faded away in vapor. Heine then continues:

How great a drama is the passion of Christ! How great a figure is this Man-God. His words are a balm for all the wounds this world can inflict; and the blood that flowed on Golgotha has become a healing stream for all who suffer. The white marble gods of the Greeks were spattered with his blood and they sickened with terror and could never more regain their health. . . . The lighthearted ancient gods, who themselves felt no pain, did not know the feelings of poor tormented humanity; and poor, tormented humanity could not turn to them in its direst need, for he who sees his own god suffer bears his own cross more easily. To be loved with the whole heart, one must have suffered; therefore of all the gods that have ever been, Christ is the most beloved, especially by women.

Aeschylus, the Greek dramatist, defines the function of

tragedy as "the purification of the emotions through pity." That mysterious quality of wonder and insight into the nature of things that shows forth in human tragedy, especially when goodness suffers, is the most appealing force in life. It is this which gives the crucifixion story its strange power over the human heart. The nail-pierced hands of Christ have not only "lifted empires off their hinges"; but, through their incomparable appeal, have been the world's most dynamic factor in creating the godly sorrow that renews the life of the race. "Again and again I have been tempted to give up the struggle," says George Tyrrell, "but always the figure of the Strange Man hanging on the Cross drives me back to my task."

In the long story of the ethical purification of the human spirit, the figure of the Strange Man on the Cross has occupied the focal point of humanity's vision. More than any other fact of history has the mysterious death of the Holy and Just One made its impact on the world; and has touched with lonely power the springs of penitence and hope in the hearts of men of every race and culture. In backward lands the crucifixion tale has been the penetrating point by which the Christian message has pierced the callousness and prejudice of heathenism; and in more advanced nations, among cultured and mighty intellects, it has carried its weight in high circles of government and at the council tables of sovereign states. It seems to be the one event in human history in which is concentrated the whole power of eternity, the thing by which God pre-eminently touched the world.

There are mysterious and illusive overtones surrounding the death of Christ that defy analysis. On the surface the story is simple as a nursery rhyme; but as one contemplates its far-reaching implications, it becomes the profoundest fact in all of man's philosophies. The little girl who once said to her pastor, "I do not understand why Jesus had to die and how his death saves me," expressed the problem that has absorbed the minds of thoughtful persons since the first century.

As we contemplate the happenings during those closing days of our Lord's life, two things stand out about his Passion: first, it is something intensely personal; and second, it is something universal. It is an event that has local meaning; it is also an event with eternal significance. It is something that happened once in history, at a certain time and place; it is something that is repeated throughout all history. Here are all the elements of the world's greatest tragedy. It is the most perfect drama on earth, with all its lights and shadows, its interplay of characters and emotions, its cross-currents of conflicting forces, all moving steadily and with irresistible momentum toward the final great tragic end. And the awesome part of it is that it is not fiction but fact. The thing really happened. The story is true.

But in any human event there are always two aspects: the fact, and the explanation of the fact. The death of Christ is one of the most solid facts of history; but the interpretation of it has varied with the thought-forms of every age that has followed. Ever since the crucifixion, Christian thinkers have wrestled with the problem of the meaning of the cross for man and have derived a host of explanations that constitute a sizeable body of the world's literature. There have been a number of major theories of the atonement that have held sway over men's minds for centuries; such as the Ransom Theory of Irenaeus in the second century, the Debt Theory of Anselm in the eleventh, the Penal Theory of the Reformers, the Governmental Theory of Hugo Grotius in the seventeenth century, and the Moral Influence Theory of Abelard. A great many lesser ones, including those of the present day, are merely modifications or derivatives of these great historical theories.

The apostles never attempted to give a clearly defined rationale of the death of Christ. They merely preached the hard-core fact that Christ died for our sins; and let the momentous event speak for itself and carry its own weight. It is true that St. Paul in his writings uses such terms as "propitiation," "redemption," and "sacrifice," but the language is impressionistic rather than contractual and the images are hardly more than mere figures of speech used to describe a saving experience in the life of the believer. But for some reason, later theologies have never been willing to take the fact simply but have attempted to construe the death of Christ into a transaction in high celestial politics by which God himself was induced to do something on behalf of man he would not otherwise have been willing to do.

Some of these theologies have been crudely false and have distorted the Christian position by representing the atoning virtue of the cross in terms of a deal between God and the Devil, or as a dichotomy between the Divine Justice and the Divine Mercy, just as though God were divided against himself. William Blake, the English poet, had this theology in mind when he described the preaching of his day by saying: "First, God the Father fetches us a blow on the head, and then Christ brings us balm for our wounds." In all of these theories of the atonement, there has never been one single explanation that has represented the mind of the whole Church. Each of them has contained a measure of truth; but none of them could exhaust the truth.

The question of the crucial mechanics of salvation has been a debatable issue in the Church's life for many centuries. But the problem is fundamentally a procedural matter and not a substantive one. A man's salvation is not dependent upon his accepting a certain view of what happened in the death of Christ. Christian faith does not rest upon a theory of theology; but upon a Person whose death has opened the gates of life to us. Theologies are not everlasting truths but merely temporary formulations about a great matter. The stars do not disappear out of the sky because astronomy changes its views. The lights of earth may flicker, but the North Star abides. Theories of the atonement come and go; but the fact of the Great Sacrifice itself, like the eternal stars, does not change.

There is an indefinable quality in the human story of the death of Christ that makes us feel that the more we know about it the less we understand it. The event itself has little to do with systematic formulations of theology. For almost two thousand years it has been mankind's most potent source of moral renewal. The gaze of the first Christians was focused upon the momentous reality with a kind of stupefaction that would not let them look for long at anything else. Present-day preaching needs to recapture the classic Christian position—not to intellectualize but to adore, not to explain but to wonder. The thing must be permitted to make its own impact upon the heart. It is not too important that we theologize about it if we keep in mind that Christ died for our sins, not to change God's attitude toward us but only to reveal it; and that in his atoning death he offered a self-sacrifice to an already self-sacrificing God. This is the heart of the matter and nothing else need concern us overmuch.

Charles Clayton Morrison writes in *The Christian Century* of March 29, 1944: "Christian faith will not let us renounce either the real humanity or the real divinity of Jesus Christ, despite the difficulties which the problem of holding them together presents to human reason. On Good Friday, they dug a hole in the earth in which was set the upright beam of the cross. But the Cross which Christian faith sees, goes down to the very center of the universe and bears aloft at this particular point in history the everlasting Reality with which man has to do. That Reality is the limitless love of God. He who hangs upon the cross is 'the Lamb slain from the foundation of the world,' God himself suffering at the hands of sinful humanity and by his forgiving love reconciling the world unto himself."

Christianity is a gospel of redemption. Its message is that men must have a Saviour; and that unless the grace of God constantly flows into human life to renew it, evil will win. There may be other inhabited worlds, as some suggest, that are contributing far more to the cosmic process than the one we are living on at the present; but we can speak with no assurance at this time of any of them. What we do know is that this blood-stained planet is not much of a credit to rational beings. What with billions of dollars spent on hydrogen bombs, guided missiles, and trips to the moon in a world where two-thirds of the population is undernourished, hungry, sick and ill-housed, the situation is not too encouraging. No wonder George Bernard Shaw called the world "the lunatic asylum of the universe."

As we look at the present world picture, Reinhold Niebuhr's penetrating analysis of sin comes to mind. We see brought out with appalling clearness two classic Christian affirmations: one, the reality of a moral order that inevitably brings to men and nations the harvest of what they sow; and the other, the reality of human sin as a diabolical fact that twists to evil uses every good we seem to gain and from which it is imperative that we be saved. On every hand we see an expression of the stupidity, selfishness, and cruelty in the world about us—innocence betrayed, weakness exploited, and strength misued for evil purposes. We feel ourselves a part of a vast social organism that overwhelms us with its evil weight. We realize that men have been hating and deceiving, stealing and lying, and violating all the high sanctities for thousands of years and that the cumulative energy of it is a part of our present existence. This is true when we look at conditions in the world about us; it is even more tragically true when we look within ourselves and feel the plague of our own heart.

The will bent to deliberate wrong represents the real and central problem of the world, and the deepest question in life for every man is this: Is there something, or Someone, that can cleanse my guilty conscience and be an active prophylactic power against evil—a present Saviour who can cover *me* with the robe of his righteousness and remove the burden of my sin-stained soul in a universe ruled by a holy God? The Scriptures throb with a sense of the tragedy of history. A whole creation is groaning and travailing in pain. A great cosmic experiment has gone wrong and demands unique and drastic rehabilitation. Only through some comprehensive and unimaginably costly venture can the Divine forces break into human history and save the experiment. It was this felt need that inspired the great ones of the past.

No one can contemplate the uneasy dreaming that fills the pages of the Old Testament without feeling that the thing troubling those early seers was a prevision of a coming Deliverer who would do for man what he is unable to do for himself. What the ancient prophets dimly envisioned became an actuality in the Incarnation. The thing that gave primitive Christianity its trembling radiance was the conviction on the part of the first Christians that a Supreme Servant of that awful and impenetrable Mystery we call God had entered into human life and "by the oblation of himself once offered," and in some manner incomprehensible to us, had affected a real change in our relation to God. "In his substance according to the flesh," says Chrysostom, "he became our brother; yet in honor he greatly differed from us, it cannot be told how much."

In the profound mystery of the Incarnation we are made aware of a Divine grace that does not abandon us to our fate, nor wait for us to repent, but does all possible to bring us to repentance. Man is shipwrecked upon the will of God, as the Barthians point out; and therefore, if we are to receive this supernatural flow of strength, the one thing we must do is to surrender our proud, helpless, and guilty selves into the hands of him who has come down to rescue us.

An editorial, called "Easter After War," that appeared in *The Times* of London, April 18, 1946, gives the gist of the matter: "Men are now slowly and painfully relearning the eternal truth that the unsupported human will can never finally prevail against sin, and therefore that unsupported human effort can never make that new world for which we long. How if a man were to hear again that he who hung on the Cross on the first Good Friday was not simply a man but the Son of God in human form? How if he were to hear that with the resurrection of Christ on the first Easter Day the full freedom of the human soul was finally attained, and that to a believer who accepts Good Friday and Easter Day in a spirit of true faith and penitence there is made available a source of spiritual strength which, however often he may fall, will raise him up again and that will finally in the depths of eternity bring him to that perfection that was in the beginning designed for him? This is the core of the Christian faith."

CHAPTER THREE

THE RESURRECTION FACT

On July 16, 1945, there flashed over a few wires the startling news that the atom had been broken and the secret of atomic fission was known. In the desert fastness of New Mexico on that date, a handful of nuclear scientists had witnessed the explosion of the world's first atom bomb. In a unique and awesome experiment, man had at last laid hold upon the primeval power that generates the sun's central heat and had opened up a new world of mystery and transcendent cosmic power, destined to alter the course of all future history.

Approximately nineteen centuries before this breathtaking operation, an event of similarly startling proportions and of even more crucial significance for the future of mankind occurred. In an obscure corner of the Roman Empire, during the reign of Tiberius Caesar and following a Jewish Passover, a rumor was whispered from mouth to mouth that an unheard of thing had happened in Jerusalem. A human resurrection had taken place. A Jewish carpenter, executed by order of the Roman procurator of Judea, had survived death and had showed himself alive to as many competent witnesses as had viewed the New Mexico test. It was this revolutionary event that gave birth to the Christian church and launched a world religion on its way.

The resurrection fact is not only the most important event in the history of Christianity; but for those who are able to grasp its universal implications, it is also the most important event in the history of the world. Easter morning marks one of those great moments of time when a new dimension of reality is projected into the thought of mankind. It is a moment greater than that when Columbus opened up a new continent or Copernicus discovered a sun-centered solar system. The importance of this cataclysmic event for the race is comparable only to the appearance of life on an inanimate world or the dawn of conscious mind. Its significance rests in the fact that for the first time in human history the immutable and universal law of death was broken and a new pattern of life emerged.

The bursting of the divine atom is the world's greatest news story. For the better part of two millennia, it has been the central affirmation of Christianity and the bedrock fact of the Christian gospel. Over 900 million people living today accept the resurrection of Jesus Christ as an article of faith and profess to believe it. On Easter Sunday, thousands of ministers preach the event from their pulpits as a fact of history; and on successive Sundays throughout the year Christian congregations all over the world stand and repeat the electric words of the great Creed: "The third day he rose from the dead."

But while the resurrection event may well be the central truth of Christian preaching and the pivotal point of human history, it is the least understood and most reluctantly accepted part of the Christian faith. The early Christians saluted each other with the greeting, "Christ is risen!," followed by the answering response, "He is risen indeed!" But in this modern age, the truth of the resurrection is not so resolutely asserted.

At the present time, a sizeable part of mankind has either never heard of the event, or seriously question its historicity. Some of these people live in the South Sea Islands, the hinterlands of Asia, or the jungles of Africa; but a considerable number are walking the streets of modern cities, and in some cases sitting in churches on Sunday morning, listening to Christian sermons. Often they are not hearing

Christian sermons; for the minister himself may have his doubts about the historic reality of the great event that brought the Christian church into existence, and will be hesitant, timid, and almost apologetic about the matter.

Is the Christian gospel of the resurrection fact or fantasy? Did Jesus Christ actually rise from the dead? Ever since the first Easter, some have answered "No," and others have answered "Yes." During the Apostolic Age, those who answered "No" were the declared enemies of Jesus; but today the lines are not so sharply drawn. In the heyday of his influence, the late literary critic, H. L. Mencken, asserted that no first-rate scientist today believed in the resurrection of Jesus Christ. As was characteristic of Mencken, he overstated his case; for even in his day there were numerous distinguished scientists throughout the world who accepted the New Testament narratives as authentic history. At the present time, however, it is true that a large number of people, including many conventional believers, look upon the resurrection story as a sort of put-up job, or a museum piece of outworn dogma.

A few years ago a questionnaire was sent out to a number of persons working in the biological and physical sciences whose reputations justified their inclusion in the then current volume of *Who's Who in America.* They were asked to express their opinion concerning the resurrection of Jesus Christ. Out of 521 potential replies, 228 responded. Of the total who replied, 36 declared their belief in the resurrection as a fact of history; 142 stated they did not believe in it; while 28 did not wish to express an opinion, and 22 did not know whether they did or not. In other words, only one out of five strongly affirmed a belief in a historic resurrection, while the rest either denied it, or were not sure.

Much of the current disbelief in the resurrection undoubtedly roots back in an unwillingness or failure to investigate the evidence. The replies to the questionnaire indicated that those who denied it had never taken the trouble to carefully examine the New Testament records that describe the event. Most of them confessed that they had never investigated the matter, or had never given the subject any serious consideration. None of them attempted to offer a theory to explain away the New Testament confidence in the resurrection.

These men in their laboratories, some of whom were professed Christians, had examined the basis of physical matter but had never investigated the evidence that supports the Christian belief in the resurrection. They were experts in mathematics and the physical sciences; but many of them were more familiar with test tubes and electrical devices than they were with the New Tesament. For this reason, they were no more qualified to pass judgment on this particular matter than any other ordinary ignoramus.

That the truth of the resurrection is not universally believed and accepted, even though it has been a matter of history for over nineteen centuries, does not alter its essential factness. Most of the important matters of science or history are only dimly apprehended by the majority of people. Indeed, if many of the basic assumptions of modern technology or theoretical physics, such as the polarity of the earth, the speed of light, or the Quantum Theory were put to the test by a vote of the majority of the world's people, the truth would doubtless lose in the election. The fact may be denied; but the truth of the matter is that the available evidence for the resurrection of Christ is as weighty as for any other major event of human history. Indeed, in some respects, the evidence is even more convincing; for, as we shall notice later, the Christian Church itself is the stupendous monument erected on the event, and stands today as the concrete and irrefutable witness of its reality.

There is a cheap, cocksure intellectualism that prevents many persons in the scientific and academic communities today from examining the evidence that supports the Christian belief in the resurrection. In fact, the theological dogmatism of the Middle Ages has been replaced by the pseudo-scientific dogmatism of today. Ironically enough, our modern sophisticates often pride themselves on their openmindedness; while at the same time are so prejudiced against the possibility of the supernatural that they are unwilling even to consider the evidence. They call to mind the associates of Galileo when he discovered the moons of Jupiter through the telescope which he had invented. According to the science of that day, there ought not to be any satellites there. When Galileo said to a skeptical scientist, "Look for yourself!," the friend replied, "What's the use of looking; I know they are not there."

It goes without saying that they who are unwilling to look need not expect to see. Either through prejudice or indolence, many persons never bother to examine the available sources and therefore remain completely unaware of the historic evidence for the resurrection. On the other hand, there are notable instances of persons who have taken the trouble to investigate the facts for themselves who have come up with startling results.

A.H. Ross, an officer in the British Air Intelligence during World War II who wrote under the pseudonym of Frank Morison, is an example of a man who vehemently denied the historic resurrection but later became convinced of its truth through personal investigation of the sources. So great was his disbelief in miracles and his aversion to anything supernatural that, even as a child when reciting the Apostles' Creed with others in the Anglican service of his home church, he would repeat the words "suffered under Pontius Pilate, was crucified, dead and buried . . ." and stop dead at this point, set his teeth tightly, and refuse to utter another word. In his adult life, Ross set out to write a debunking book on the resurrection, thereby showing up Christians as a bunch of credulous fools. But he never completed the book. Instead, he went to Jerusalem to investigate the facts for himself and study the Christian background of the story. After several years of intensive investigation, he was compelled by the sheer weight of evidence to alter his position. He ended up by writing the most convicing argument for the truth of the resurrection ever written, namely, *Who Moved the Stone?*

The late C. S. Lewis of Magdalene College, Oxford, is another noted example of a man completely skeptical of the Christian claims, but who later shed his agnosticism and became one of the most able advocates of the Christian position in the English-speaking world. There are numerous other instances of doughty doubters who, at first, denied the resurrection truth but were later convinced of its reality by the strength and stubbornness of the facts themselves. But in all such cases, it was necessary to approach the subject with an openminded attitude and a willingness to follow the evidence wherever it might lead without *a priori* prejudice.

What are the historic reasons for believing in the resurrection of Jesus Christ? How did faith in it originally arise? When one examines the facts adequately and without prejudice, he will come to see that the resurrection story is no poetic legend that sprang out of the soil of primitive superstition, but is grounded in authentic history and supported by evidence strong and weighty. Like the trunk roots of a tree, there are four hard-core, indisputable facts that support the resurrection belief and from which it originally sprang:

(a) The fact of the empty tomb.

(b) The word of Jesus himself.

(c) The testimony of post-crucifixion witnesses.

(d) The existence of the Christian Church.

Let us consider these four points in the above order. The first basic reason for a belief in the resurrection is the witness of the open sepulchre. Canon Liddon called the empty tomb "the central sanctuary of the Christian faith" and said that no spot on earth has so much to say to the Christian faith as does the tomb of Christ.

When the women came to the sepulchre on Easter morning, bringing spices to anoint the body of Jesus, all four of the gospels relate that they found the body gone and the tomb vacant. This fact stands out with stark and imperishable clearness in all the Christian sources of the first and second centuries, including not only the New Testament but also that massive body of apocryphal writings in the years that followed. In all the extant literature of that early period, there is no suggestion of controversy at this point. From the moment the women made their breathtaking discovery, through all the early decades of Christianity, the physical vacancy of the tomb seems to have been taken for granted. As to this matter, enemies of Jesus as well as his friends were in complete agreement. The issue was never as to whether the grave of Jesus was empty, only the vexed question as to why it was empty.

The fact of the open tomb has been subject to the most searching and critical analysis of any event in history. Biblical rationalists of the nineteenth and early twentieth centuries went to great lengths to disprove the evidence for it. Many and ingenious were their explanations. One view put forth was that of the French rationalist, C. H. Guignebert, for many years professor at the University of Paris, to the effect that the tomb of Joseph was empty simply because the body of Jesus was never placed there. Guignebert contended that the body of Jesus, together with the two criminals who were crucified with him, was thrown into a ditch. However, he does not give a single shred of evidence for his theory.

Ancient and modern questioners have racked their brains in an attempt to explain away this stubborn bit of history and to provide a plausible alternative to the gospel thesis. Every conceivable solution to the riddle has been suggested at some time. Some of the theories have been so fantastic as to border on the humorous; and, from a logical standpoint, would hardly be worth considering were it not for the fact that at one time or another they have been put forward by a few serious-minded scholars. Most of them have had their innings and are now little more than historical curiosities.

Three of the most important of these have been known as the Swoon Theory, the Hallucination Theory, and the Fraud Theory. In general, practically all of the views that seek to give a strictly rationalistic explanation of the post-crucifixion phenomena during the past century and a half would fall under one of these three headings. All of them are now obsolete. However, they are still sometimes put forward by uninformed persons as arguments against a historic resurrection. The Swoon Theory held that Jesus did not really die on the cross but only fainted from loss of blood and exhaustion and later revived in the tomb and came forth. The Hallucination, or Vision Theory, contended that Christ did not rise from the grave; his followers only imagined that he did because of a vision seen by one or more of his disciples. The Fraud Theory carried the argument that the first apostles themselves falsified the evidence and thus invented the Easter story.

The first of these theories, which was originally put forward by the German rationalist Venturini, suggests that the death of Christ was only a delayed coma; that Jesus did not die on the cross but only fainted, and later in the cool temperature of the grave he recovered and subsequently appeared to his disciples. The documentary evidence is so overwhelmingly against this view, however, that few persons take it seriously today. The theory has long since been abandoned and lies buried in its grave without hope of resurrection. The evidence of the records is that Jesus was truly dead. The author of the Fourth Gospel specifically states that a spear was thrust into Jesus' side; and that he was pronounced dead by the Roman officer who supervised the execution. It is hardly likely that Roman soldiers, who were experts in the grim art of killing, would not know when they had completed their job.

A further weakness of the resuscitation theory is that even if Jesus had revived after his ordeal on the cross, it would have been humanly impossible for him to have come forth from the tomb on his own strength. It is unthinkable that a half-dead man could extricate himself from the grave-wrappings that, in accordance with the burial customs of that day, bound him, roll away a huge stone that had challenged the strength of three women; do this from the inside of a sealed sepulchre; and then escape unnoticed by a guard of Roman soldiers.

The resuscitation theory was given its *coup de grâce* a century ago by the great German philosopher David Strauss, himself a disbeliever in the resurrection, when he wrote his book *The Life of Jesus.* "It is impossible," says Strauss, "that a being who had stolen half-dead out of the sepulchre, who crept about weak and ill, wanting medical treatment, who required bandaging, strengthening and indulgence, and who still at last yielded to his sufferings, could have given the disciples the impression that he was a Conqueror over death and the grave, the Prince of Life, an impression which lay at the bottom of their future ministry."

The second, or Vision Theory, held that the original belief in the resurrection was founded on a delusion. The disciples *thought* that something had happened; but they were mistaken. The whole thing was simply a subjective phenomenon, like the false dagger in the heat-oppressed brain of Macbeth, without any foundation in objective reality. According to this view, the disciples were in an excitable condition, eager to grasp at any evidence that their Master was still alive. A group of women go to the tomb in an early hour of the morning and see the white grave-clothes, and in their hysteric state of mind imagine they have seen the risen Saviour. Renan, the French critic, taunted the believers of his day by saying, "You Christians pin your faith on the fragrance of an empty vase", and suggested that it was the "strong imagination" of Mary Magdalene that gave the world the idea of "a resuscitated God."

An obvious fallacy of this theory is that it contradicts all the available evidence. It is built on the belief that the friends of Jesus confidently expected the resurrection; whereas the very reverse of this is true. The thing was wholly unexpected and came as a complete surprise. The women who came to the tomb to embalm the body of Jesus were upset to find it empty. When they reported the fact to the others, "their words seemed to them as idle tales." It was necessary for

Jesus on a number of occasions to go to great lengths to overcome their incredulity. The records are clear that the followers of Jesus were as little disposed to believe the resurrection story at the time it happened as would be the most skeptical materialist today. It was only after overwhelming proof that they finally came to accept it.

Furthermore, the hallucination view is inadequate to explain the strength of the disciples' witness, which they later made at such damaging costs to themselves. "I readily believe," wrote Pascal, "those witnesses who get their throats cut." The terrors and persecutions the early Christians ultimately faced with such unflinching courage do not admit of a half-hearted belief secretly honeycombed with doubt. A belief such as theirs would need something far more tangible to support it than the mere psychological repercussion of a woman's dream. Men do not ordinarily take desperate risks on the strength of such fragile things, or give their lives for a belief that is less than adamantine in its certainty.

The third, or Fraud Theory, was that the early Christians falsified the evidence. It is difficult to understand how such a theory could have been seriously entertained. The suggestion was made in apostolic times by the enemies of Jesus that the disciples had stolen or abducted his body and then spread the report that he had risen. But the universal moral sense and feeling of mankind has rejected their claim as preposterous. It is repugnant and contradictory to the known ethical qualities of the disciples. They were not the kind of people to do something like this. As someone has suggested, "Christianity as a moral phenomenon could not have been built upon rottenness." Furthermore, the question raised centuries ago by the Roman writer Tertullian is still pertinent: "Will men willingly die for the sake of a story they know to be false?" It is hardly likely that the apostles would have accepted martyrdom in order to perpetuate what they knew to be a gigantic hoax. The unassailable logic of this fact has long since demolished the theory; and not a single writer whose work is of critical value today would now hold that the claim of fraud has a single leg on which to stand.

Such fanciful theories as the above only go to show the extremes men will sometimes go in an effort to explain away what to them is an unwelcome fact. The assumption of the anti-miraculists often seems to be that they are free from the obligation, binding on all other historians, to support their arguments with proof. Despite the superficial appearance of rationality their views sometimes carry, all of them have one fatal weakness—they offer no positive explanation as to why the disciples believed in the resurrection.

It is easy to see the annihilating character of the evidence available to Jesus' enemies by simply producing the body of Jesus and thereby refuting the claims of his disciples that he had risen. We need to remember that Joseph of Arimathea's sepulchre was only a fifteen-minute walk outside the walls of the old city of Jerusalem. All that would have been necessary to disprove the disciples' story was for the priestly authorities to lead a procession down to the grave, break the seals, and make an extended exhibition of the remains. This would have ended all argument and decisively closed the case. But this was never done. And the fact that it was not done is a highly significant factor in the case.

The strange paralysis of the Jewish leaders is an intriguing psychological phenomenon. If Caiaphas and the Jewish hierarchy, who were so furious at the apostles' preaching of the resurrection, could have easily silenced that preaching but did not do so, why did they not? It is clear that the Christians could never have preached successfully, or even at all, in the presence of the physical remains of Jesus. Yet the indisputable fact is that they not only preached it but preached it so effectively that converts were made to Christianity at a spectacular rate.

According to the description in the Book of Acts of what happened at Pentecost, three thousand persons were converted to Christianity in a single day, with the number increasing phenomenally in the weeks and months that followed. We are also told that included in the number of these new converts was "a great company of priests who were obedient to the faith" (Acts 6:7), suggesting that the new religion was making inroads into the opposition's camp with devastating effectiveness. All of this took place in Jerusalem, less than two months after the crucifixion, and within a few hundred yards of the place where the body of Jesus had been entombed. By the sheer logic of circumstances it is reasonable to conclude that the reason the enemies of Jesus did not produce his body was that there was no body to be produced; and thus it was that the physical vacancy of the tomb constituted a positive and unassailable argument for the resurrection that could not be gainsaid or denied.

The second basic reason for believing in a historic resurrection is what Jesus himself said about it. Christians have come to accept some things on the basis of their confidence in the infallibility of Jesus and the integrity of his spoken word. Since his authority is unquestioned in spiritual matters, it is logical to infer that any statement of fact he might make would be equally justified and trustworthy. A character so self-consistent, so sane and mentally balanced as Jesus was, is not given to foolish or irrational utterances. The author of the Sermon on the Mount was not the kind of person to make boastful or irresponsible statements about himself. Yet if there is one solid, tangible, and incontrovertible fact in the New Testament, it is that Jesus had a premonition or foreknowledge of his survival of death and spoke of it a number of times before it took place.

The positive and definite assertion that after three days he would rise again occurs in all of the gospels and is among the best attested portion of the inspired records. As an example, let us take a single passage from the Gospel of Mark, the oldest and most authoritative of the sources: "And he began to teach them, that the Son of Man must suffer many things, and be rejected of the elders, and of the chief priests, and scribes, and be killed, and after three days rise again." (8:31) Five times in Mark's gospel alone the solemn warning of his death is repeated; and in each case, there invariably follows the definite assertion that after his death he will rise again. The author of St. John's gospel and the Synoptic writers are equally explicit at this point. Like the motif of a great *symphonie pathétique*, the phrase, "after three days" is repeated throughout the gospel narratives and becomes more frequent and unmistakable as Jesus approaches the end of his career.

A number of times members of Jesus' inner circle were thrown into perplexity and confusion over the saying. Once following this statement by their Master, we are told that the disciples questioned in their minds "what the rising from the dead should mean"; and on a later occasion, the account states that "they understood not the saying and were afraid to ask him." The prophesy, however, was not confined to the inner circle but seems to have been spoken in public as well. That it had become a matter of public knowledge is borne out by the fact that, following the crucifixion, the chief priests are recorded as coming to Pilate and asking for a guard at the tomb, saying, "Sir, we remember that this deceiver said, while he was yet alive, After three days I will rise again." (Mt. 27:63)

The fact that Jesus predicted his own resurrection would not of itself prove that the thing actually took place. It does, however, furnish contributory evidence of the highest order; particularly when we remember that the prediction itself was an important part of the case against him in the trial before the Jewish authorities. Out of the confused and conflicting testimony of that eventful night, this clear-cut and positive bit of evidence emerged as the major indictment against Jesus; namely, that he was heard to state before a number of witnesses that he would destroy the temple of God and in three days would build it again. In his record of the trial, St. Matthew says:

"At the last came two false witnesses, and said: This fellow said, I am able to destroy the temple of God, and to build it in three days." (26:60)

According to St. Mark's account, the accusation of the witnesses was even stronger; that Jesus not only claimed the power to do so but had deliberately threatened to destroy the temple and replace it magically in three days. The words are quite explicit:

"And there arose certain, and bore false witness against him, saying: We heard him say, I will destroy this temple that is made with hands, and within three days I will build another made without hands." (14:57)

What was the historic utterance that lay behind this charge against Jesus? It is difficult to believe that he would ever have made a claim so fantastic as that attributed to him by his enemies. Consider its implications. Jesus is made to say that by his own power and volition he could magically replace the Temple of Herod, which had been in the process of building for forty-six years, by pulling it down, or causing it to disappear, and rebuilding it within three days. Such an event could only have been brought about by the exercise of supernormal or magical powers beyond anything ever asserted of Christ and comparable only to the most high-handed conjuration of some character out of *The Arabian Nights*. No really sane person, especially one of the moral and intellectual caliber of Jesus, would ever have made such a grotesque and overweening boast about his own powers. Yet it is impossible to think that an accusation so manifestly absurd could ever have been seriously brought forth as the gravamen of a charge on which to successfully bring judgment against a man on trial for his life.

Did these men deliberately invent the charge or were they merely perverting to their own purpose an actual and somewhat similar statement of Christ? Under the circumstances it is hard to believe that so definite and incriminating a statement was pure invention. Since it is easier and more natural to misinterpret the words of another than to lie outright against him, it seems more likely that the case against Jesus was based on a garbled account of something his enemies had heard him say, rather than a false accusation simply drawn out of the air. Certain people might be willing to twist the truth, but only the most brazen will voice approval of a deliberate and calculated lie. For this reason, it would seem logical to hold that Jesus did upon some definite occasion use words closely resembling those with which he was charged. Indeed, there is a very positive bit of documentary evidence to this effect.

According to the author of the Fourth Gospel, the incident in question took place in the temple courts when Jesus expelled the Jewish merchants who were making a bazaar of the house of God. The priests naturally objected to this high-handed expulsion. They asked him by what right he should take command of the temple courts, of which they were the official custodians, and challenged him to give them a sign to substantiate his authority. In reply, Jesus is recorded as making the cryptic statement, "Destroy this temple and in three days I will raise it up," and the writer adds parenthetically, "But he spake of the temple of his body." In other words, what Jesus seems to have said on this occasion, and which was given an obvious but wrong interpretation by his enemies, was something more extraordinary and unbelievable than his claims of the magical replacement of the temple. In effect he was saying, "If you kill me, I will rise from the dead."

But not only did Jesus speak publicly of his ensuing resurrection; but the records are quite clear that he seriously laid plans for the event in advance with his disciples. One of the most unique promises ever given to a group of people on earth is described as having been made at the Last Supper. St. Mark records it in these strange and incredible words:

"And Jesus saith unto them. All ye shall be offended because of me this night: for it is written, I will smite the shepherd, and the sheep shall be scattered. But after that I am risen, *I will go before you into Galilee.*" (14:27)

70

St. Matthew relates that after the resurrection the eleven disciples went away into Galilee to "a mountain where Jesus had appointed them." (28:16) In other words, according to the two Evangelists, prior to his crucifixion Jesus had made a definite promise to meet his disciples in Galilee following his death and had actually specified a certain mountain, whose name and location they doubtless all knew, on which the meeting would take place. Never before in history has such an unheard-of engagement as this been made or kept; yet if we accept the gospel records as authentic, we must give credence to the words.

This sublime intuition of Jesus regarding his death and resurrection is one of the most impressive facts of the gospel narratives. How did he know he would rise the third day? We may not say. It is one of those mysteries surrounding the person of Christ that we cannot penetrate; yet the actuality of the prediction is as present a fact in the gospels as that of the cross itself. To discount or deny the historicity of the one makes it necessary to discount the reality of the other as well. Just as Phidias, the Greek sculptor, interwove his name into the shield of Minerva so that it could not be removed without destroying the shield, the prophesy of Jesus concerning his survival of death is so much an integral part of the written records that it cannot be removed or denied without destroying confidence in the entire gospel witness on every other matter as well.

There does not seem to be any hermeneutical principle whereby the ethical teachings of Jesus can be separated from his teaching concerning himself. The same lips that taught us to love one another and to pray "Our Father," claimed unmistakably that after three days he would rise again. Could he be so right in his ethical teachings and so wrong in his judgment on overt matters? If the resurrection did not take place, we are shut up to two possible alternatives. Either Jesus thought he would rise from the dead, and was mistaken; or else he knew he would not rise from the dead, but wanted his disciples and the public to think so. In the first case, he reveals himself as completely irresponsible and untrustworthy. In the second, if he knew he would not rise from the dead but attempted to make others believe he would, then he was a deceiver of the most despicable sort. We are thus forced into the intolerable position that if Jesus did not rise from the dead, he was either a deceiver or mentally off the beam. In either case, the structure of Christian faith built upon confidence in his person crumbles; and his words must remain for all time the heartbreaking mockery of the world's most deluded incompetent.

A third proof of the resurrection is the testimony of the post-crucifixion witnesses. No amount of historical skepticism can get rid of the fact that in the first century there arose a small but aggressive society of men and women who believed that they were in the service of a Person who had died and lived again. This conviction was rooted in the testimony of their senses. They believed in his continued existence because they claimed to have seen him and spoken with him after his crucifixion. There are those who may doubt the fact of the resurrection; but no one seriously questions the primitive *belief* in the fact. The reality of this conviction is one of the most definite and unassailably attested certainties of history. As one scholar put it, "It is easier, even for a non-believer in miracles, to accept the fact of the resurrection than to find any other adequate explanation of the change that came over the disciples within three days after they fled from Jerusalem."

How was it that the followers of Jesus came to believe in this astonishing thing? The easy assumption of supercilious critics is that they were a deluded bunch of people, doubtless victims of collective hallucination. This itself is a prodigious assumption. Highly neurotic individuals, in rare instances, are known to have been victims of hallucinatory states of mind; but not whole groups of people, and particularly not the kind of people we are considering—practical-minded fishermen, tax collectors and down-to-earth common people. That five hundred persons of this sort on one occasion fell under the spell of delusion is quite unthinkable.

But when the smugly self-satisfied skeptic has easily explained to his own satisfaction how the deluded disciples individually came to believe that Jesus had risen, there still remains the much weightier matter that requires attention: Granted that the friends of Jesus themselves believed in his resurrection, how did they manage to convince others of this fact? It might have been possible, even though highly unlikely, for a few credulous people to privately nurse the opinion that Jesus had survived death; but the task of convincing others of this truth is a more formidable undertaking. Even though the practical, unimaginative fisherman like the Apostle Peter, the characteristically doubting Thomas, and every other member of the party of Jesus were naive enough to believe such an absurd thing as a human resurrection, how was it possible to convert others to its truth, particularly persons previously hostile to Jesus and his ministry? We need to remember that when we have accounted for the belief of the disciples we must also account for the sudden and phenomenal rise of Christianity.

The resurrection story that was circulated throughout the ancient world during the first forty years of the Christian era was not taught or preached by outsiders, but by the original band of the followers of Jesus. They did not wait several decades before giving their version to the world, thus opening up possibilities for legendary accretions to develop; they openly declared it contemporaneously to the event itself. The first public affirmation of the resurrection of Jesus was made during the Feast of Weeks—that is to say, the Feast immediately following the Passover, less than two months after the crucifixion. This preaching did not take place in far-off Galilee, but in the capital city of Jerusalem, the stronghold of political and religious authority and the center of organized opposition to the new movement. With inconceivable audacity, the disciples carried their story into the very heart of the enemy's camp; and within seven weeks of the crucifixion began publicly preaching the fact that their

Master had risen, and did this within five hundred yards of his vacant tomb.

The results were phenomenal. As we have already noticed, a great number of the priestly caste became Christians as a result of the apostles' preaching. Indeed, it eventually turned out that the weightiest single witness of the resurrection was not from the inner circle of Jesus' friends, but from his enemies; a man violently hostile to the disciples of Jesus, who set out to smash the Christian movement but was finally engulfed by it. The conversion of Saul of Tarsus cannot be explained in terms of "atmospherics," womanly hysteria, or the morbid imaginations of a few people. The logic of the situation will not stand even a small part of the historic strain such a view puts upon it.

Here is a man of acute and powerful intellect, a Roman citizen by birth, thoroughly educated in both Jewish and Greek learning, a person of tremendous moral convictions, a great man of his age and one who eventually helped to shape all the Christian centuries. Highly endowed by nature and with advantages possessed by few, Saul was passionately devoted to the religion of his fathers. At the time of his conversion, he was a powerful agent of the ecclesiastical organization and had risen to a position of importance among his people. For some extraordinary reason, this man surrenders his position of power and casts in his lot with the hated followers of the Nazarene. He throws away the favor of the mighty and the good will of his own people to join with those whom he had been persecuting; to worship the name of Jesus which previously had been abhorrent to him; and to begin a ministry whose hazards, hardships, and accomplishments have rarely been equalled by any other man.

How did it happen that one of the most powerful intellects of his age was brought over from one pole of dogmatic belief to its opposite; who suddenly changed from being the most zealous enemy of the Christian movement to become the most ardent and energetic of all the followers of

Jesus? What personal advantage did such a man have to obtain by preaching the resurrection? What gain or glory could he hope to reap from it? Indeed, what did any of that great company of martyrs who marched in the vanguard of the early Christian movement hope to gain by their testimony?

While his enemies crushed him with stones, Stephen, the first Christian martyr, died with an unearthly serenity on his face, testifying he had seen the risen Lord; a few years later, James the Just was beheaded for the same testimony; eventually the Apostle Peter suffered martyrdom for the faith; and the Man of Tarsus went to the ends of the earth for the Christ he had originally hated. Within a matter of three decades after the apostles had begun to preach the resurrection, most of them had perished violently for their adherence to the story.

What was the explanation for the unwavering testimony of these men, and why did they make it at such a cost to themselves? The only logical answer is that they made it because it was the solemn truth. They told the story because it was the only story that truthful people could tell. It was indisputable fact. It was the way the thing had happened, and their witness has come down to us today as irrefutable evidence for the resurrection because it vibrates with the reality of historic truth.

Added to the witness of the empty tomb, confidence in the word of Jesus, and the testimony of the apostles, a fourth great reason for the belief in the resurrection is the existence of the Christian Church. Someone has observed that the resurrection of Jesus Christ is the best attested fact of history because the whole Church bears witness to it. As Professor C. H. Dodd suggests, it is a mistake to assume that the whole course of Christian history is "a massive pyramid balanced on the apex of some trivial occurrence." Some great cause is necessary to explain the Church's origin. The resurrection was the trigger-pulling event, the Noetic thing, that gave birth to the Christian religion; and without it, the Church would never have come into existence in the first place. If Jesus had survived death only in an existential sense, with a physical body deteriorating in the tomb, no one would have believed in his continued life and the early Christian movement would have aborted at its inception.

All the records support the position that despite the Master's repeated warnings of his approaching death, the disciples were wholly unprepared for the crucifixion and what followed it. At first we see them crushed and bewildered by the death of their Leader, almost in a state of panic. They mourn as for one hopelessly dead and are fearful of their lives. But within a matter of a few days, a miraculous change takes place within the group. Their despair has given away to joy; and their cowardice has been replaced by a contagious boldness. From crushed and trembling men, they become radiant preachers who go into many cities, and in the face of opposition and persecution give fearless witness to a new gospel. Within one generation, this group has carried its message to the farthest bounds of the West, and the new religion has begun to disturb the peace of the Roman Empire itself.

What was it that produced this radical change within them? The only logical answer is the resurrection. The disciples were convinced that they had met Jesus alive after his passion; and the only rational explanation of their conviction is that they were right. Each successive generation seems to make it less and less probable that this tremendous human experience could be based on pure illusion. If it be an illusion, then it is perhaps the most gloriously creative, the most lasting and far-reaching illusion that has ever possessed the minds of men; and has had infinitely greater effect on the course of human history than any attested fact.

Niagara Falls leaps to its grandeur because it has behind it the pressure of four mighty lakes. Such consequences as have sprung out of the apostolic message could not be based on fraud or fancy but must have behind them the push of some great event. The disciples believed and preached that God had raised Jesus from the dead. On the strength of that belief, they became transformed men. It was this fontal source of apostolic faith which brought the Christian Church into existence and sent it singing down the centuries. It was this fact that originated the early Christian practice of observing the first day of the week as the one on which the Master had risen from the grave, and thus eventually changed the time-honored and jealously-guarded Jewish Sabbath into the Christian Sunday. It was this belief that sent the Church's martyrs to the stake and its missionaries to the ends of the earth. And finally, it was the ultimate impact of this new faith that split the centuries and divided human history into the two categories of *before* and *after* Christ. All these things call for some great predisposing cause. The only fact revealed in the pages of the New Testament powerful enough to create such results was the overwhelming conviction on the part of the early Christians that Jesus who was crucified had survived bodily death.

The superstructure of Christianity was not reared upon "the fragrance of an empty vase"; but upon something far more tangible and historic. The fact of the resurrection of Jesus Christ, like a great rock jutting far out in the ocean, was the foundation of that great body of literature which we call the New Testament. It has been embodied in the great historic creeds, voiced in the thrilling music of the church from the simple hymns of Wesley and Watts to the stupendous masses of Bach and Beethoven, enshrined in its glorious art and massive architecture, central for nineteen centuries in its varied liturgy, its sacraments, and its rich symbolism, and constituting the supreme climax of its essential genius and message. Like the sound of many waters may be heard the voice of an invisible multitude throughout the centuries chanting the historic faith of Christendom, *Et resurrexit tertia die secundum Scriptures*—"And the third day he rose again according to the Scriptures."

CHAPTER FOUR

THE MANNER OF THE RESURRECTION

The substance of apostolic preaching was not simply Jesus, but Jesus *and the resurrection.* Originally an "apostle" was a man who had seen and talked with Jesus after his crucifixion and could testify to that fact. So integral a part of the total message of first-century Christianity was the resurrection truth, that when Paul preached to the Greeks at Athens they thought he was proclaiming two new gods—Jesus and Anastasis (Resurrection).

Modern scholarship accepts the fact that something highly exceptional took place following the death of Jesus that gave birth to the early church and launched the Christian movement. Evidence for this is so overwhelming that it is impossible for any thoughtful person to deny the fact. But the big question that divides present-day theologians is the nature of the event itself. What actually took place following the crucifixion? Interpretations differ widely at this point. Some accept the Easter Faith but deny the Easter Fact from which the faith was derived, which is a little like trying to keep the light after putting out the lamp. In general there are three viewpoints concerning the nature of the resurrection events:

The first of these, represented by the philosophical and psychological "theologies" with which we have been deluged the past few years, is that the resurrection was not an actual happening in the physical world but only a subjective experience on the part of the first disciples. The men who hold this position regard the Easter story as a myth or allegory and maintain that the reports of Jesus' appearances to his followers were merely "the legendary concretizing of the faith of the early church."

According to this view, the resurrection is not a literal fact but only the vehicle of an idea. Jesus did not actually return from the grave; he rose in the *kerygma* and is present only where the word that testifies to him is proclaimed. Existential theology has thus substituted an ontological concept for historic reality and has replaced the Jesus of history with the Christ of dogma.

A disturbing thing about the vocabulary of the de-mythologizers is that it is often hard to say just exactly what these learned gentlemen are driving at. There is an apparent inability on their part to communicate their ideas intelligibly; not only to the ordinary layman who may have difficulty understanding their philosophical subtleties, but to other scholars as well. They use the traditional Christian vocabulary but employ it in the loose way of Humpty Dumpty, who said, "When I use a word, it means what I choose it to mean, nothing more or less." Especially at the point of the resurrection event are they prone to be evasive and guilty of theological double talk.

Such persons claim to be Christian in their presentation and yet they deny the basic truth that gave rise to the Christian belief. Their historic sense is too sound to permit them to assert that nothing happened at Easter; and yet their prejudices against the supernatural will not let them admit that such an event as a resurrection could have occurred. And so they remain suspended between two poles of thought, trying strenuously to have their theological cake and eat it at the same time, which is a little difficult to manage. Many of their efforts go beyond de-mythologization and become de-factualization.

To treat the crucifixion as history and the resurrection as myth is an absurd reading of the New Testament records. There is no difference between the reality and the actuality of the crucifixion and that of the resurrection. Each possesses the same degree of historicity. To deny the one, logically we must deny the other also. When the gospel is thus divorced from history and identified with a complex of metaphysical ideas, what it ought to be called is hardly worth discussing, but that it is not historic Christianity is quite clear.

At the opposite pole from those who transmute the resurrection into a purely psychological event, are those who unthinkingly regard the resurrection as merely the resuscitation of the dead body of Jesus to a state of existence identical to that experienced before his crucifixion. A recent issue of a church publication by a theologically conservative denomination carried an article written by one of its leaders expressing this view. A few sentences will reveal the argument:

Our Lord Jesus Christ today has a physical body as real as when he was on earth. This body has flesh and bones as he himself said it had after the resurrection (Luke 24:59). In his human body he went into heaven (Acts 1:11) and has been living in heaven for nearly two thousand years. He will live and plead for us there (Hebrews 7:25) until he comes again in the same body to gather his own to himself.

In contending for the historic truth of an authentic resurrection over against those who would deny its objective reality, it is not necessary to go to the opposite extreme, as the above writer does, and attempt to maintain the unscriptural position of the resurrection of the flesh. This would be merely re-animation and not resurrection, which is something quite different from that which the first Christians gave witness. In his great analogy of the seed in the fifteenth chapter of Corinthians, the Apostle Paul emphatically declares that flesh and blood cannot inherit the Kingdom of God and that the resurrection body is not the old flesh restored, but is as different from the old as the new plant is different from the sown seed that produced it. Since the emphasis of the New Testament upon the return of Jesus from the dead is upon personal survival and continuity and not upon physical identity, it is more accurate to speak of a *personal* rather than a *physical* resurrection.

The third view is that the resurrection was not merely a subjective event, nor the resuscitation of a corpse, but that it was something distinctively different from either. In the phenomenon of Jesus' risen life, the records are quite clear that the "pneumatic" body of the resurrection was something strikingly different to that which hung on the cross and was laid in the tomb. While it was so objectively real as to have exerted an external force and to have remained existent even though no witnesses had been present, yet it was essentially non-material in its nature.

The late Karl Barth, at the forefront of leading contemporary theologians, emphasizes this aspect when he points out the fact that in all other stories of resurrection, death has never been transcended. It had merely been postponed. Unlike the case of Lazarus, who returned to the old life apparently subject to his previous material limitations and destined to experience a second death, the return of Christ from the grave was of an entirely different order. It was a higher mode of existence in which his body possessed strange and unheard-of powers, or rather became independent of earthly limitations.

During the forty days following his crucifixion, Jesus seems to have become clothed with new and transcendent powers of action, not hitherto possessed. The ordinary laws of physical existence no longer limit him. He passes through closed doors as no mere physical body could do. Time and space no longer hinder his movements. He appears in different localities considerable distances apart, seemingly at will. He does not go away from his disciples. He merely vanishes. He does not come to them. He simply "stands in their midst."

Also, he reveals mysterious powers by which he could assume a temporary disguise so that those who had been his closest associates are unable to recognize him until a familiar gesture, look or tell-tale inflection of voice reveal his identity to them. Mary Magdalene recognizes him by the way he calls her name; John, when he showed the disciples how to fish; Thomas, by the appearance on the Lord's body of the mystic stigmata of his crucifixion; while the two Emmaus disciples walked several miles with him without recognizing him until he made himself known to them in the act of blessing and breaking the bread.

The evidence in the gospels overwhelmingly indicates that Jesus' resurrected body was not a natural body or a phantom, but something quite different. The conventional pattern of thought is that there are only two possible modes of being, one entirely spiritual and the other entirely physical. But the New Testament documents suggest the existence of a third—a higher mode of being which partakes of the characteristics of *both* pure spirit *and* pure body, an order of life which retains its complete human identity and yet manifests powers and qualities that transcend the plane of the human.

This fact is brought out not only in the canonical writings, but in later Christian literature as well. In an old second-century document called the Acts of John, there is a curious passage which doubtless reflects an ancient memory of the forty days. John the Apostle is relating his experience of Jesus to the others, and says: "Sometimes when I would lay hold upon him, I met with a material and solid body, and at other times, again, when I felt him, the substance was immaterial and as if it existed not at all."

It was this exceptional quality in the risen form of Jesus that seemed to disturb and puzzle the first disciples. The writers of these early records give the impression of trying to describe something they did not have either the experience or the vocabulary to interpret. These records reflect the artless honesty of men who have stumbled on to something so unlike anything they had known before as to leave them mystified and confused. They seem to be saying, "These are the facts: make what you can of them." In the case of Lazarus, his return to life was accepted or rejected immediately; but the fact of the risen Christ was of a wholly different sort and met with only a reluctant and puzzled acceptance. St. Paul was still struggling with the problem many years after the event. "There is a natural body," he said, "and there is a spiritual body."

In the light of the foregoing facts, it is idle to talk of the resurrection of Christ as though it were merely the case of a dead man returned to life. Here is a mode of being radically different to the ordinary human level of existence. Clearly a body with powers to resist gravity, to make itself visible or invisible at will, at times to appear quite physical and at other times to be immaterial, is on the verge of escaping into a timeless sphere where all earthly limitations are superseded.

Biblical scholarship is under a debt of gratitude to the late Dr. Henry Latham of England for the valuable study of the great forty days contained in his book, *The Risen Master.* This modest little volume, written at the beginning of the century by the gifted Master of Trinity College, Cambridge, is a priceless gem of insight into the nature of the resurrection and is as fresh and readable as when it was first written.

After making a searching critical analysis of the original Greek in the passage from John's Gospel describing the visit of Peter and John to the tomb, Latham reaches the conclusion that the author of the Fourth Gospel was trying to convey to us that there was something peculiar and deeply significant in the way the grave-clothes were lying—something that gave the unmistakable impression that they had not been touched by human hands after being placed in the tomb; but that in some mysterious manner unknown to us at the present time, the body of Jesus had been withdrawn from them without disturbing the original wrappings.

To understand Latham's thesis, one needs to recall that in the ancient Jewish custom of preparing a corpse for burial, the body was usually bandaged tightly from the armpits to the ankles by strips of cloth about a foot wide. Aromic spices, often of a gummy nature, were placed between the strips of linen. These served partially as a preservative and partially as cement to glue the wrappings into a solid covering. When the body was thus enveloped, a separate cloth was wrapped about the head and tied under the chin to prevent the lower jaw from sagging. The face and neck of the corpse were therefore left uncovered, so that between the grave-clothes and the turban there was the space of almost a foot left wholly bare.

It was doubtless in some such manner as this that the body of Jesus was clothed and laid in Joseph's new tomb. If, through some unknown process, the Master's body had quietly disintegrated and vanished and he himself assumed a purely spiritual existence, leaving the grave-clothes flat on the stone ledge of the sepulchre while the turban itself still retained its original annular shape as though the head had slipped out without disarranging its form, then we should have the picture which the author holds must have greeted the two apostles as they caught their first glimpse of the open tomb.

To feel the weight of this argument, let us examine carefully the passage from John's Gospel, keeping in mind that the great apostle was not attempting to describe the actual rising of Jesus from the dead, which no one is recorded to have witnessed, but instead was relating how the two disciples themselves were first convinced that the resurrection had taken place:

Now on the first day of the week Mary Magdalene came to the tomb early, while it was still dark, and saw that the stone had been taken away from the tomb. So she ran, and went to Simon Peter and the other disciple, the one whom Jesus loved, and said to them, "They have taken the Lord out of the tomb, and we do not know where they have laid him." Peter then came out with the other disciple, and they went toward the tomb. They both ran, but the other disciple outran Peter and reached the tomb first; and stooping to look in, he saw the linen cloths lying there, but he did not go in. Then Simon Peter came, following him, and went into the tomb; he saw the linen cloths lying, and the napkin, which had been on his head, not lying with the linen cloths but rolled up in a place by itself. Then the other disciple, who reached the tomb first, also went in, and he saw and believed; for as yet they did not know the scripture, that he must rise from the dead. Then the disciples went back to their homes. (John 20:1-10)

In this passage, one can hardly fail to notice the odd and repeated emphasis upon the position of the grave-clothes in the phrase, "saw the linen clothes lying." The Greek word *keimena,* which is translated "lying," is placed in the sentence in such a way as to give it the strongest possible meaning. If one wished to express the fact that it was the position of the clothes which was the striking thing in the picture, the words would be placed in just their present order. Indeed, if the intention had not been to underscore this meaning, the word "lying" would have been quite superfluous in the sentence. It would have been sufficient to have merely said, "He saw the linen clothes." This emphasis on the position of the wrappings is again reiterated in the sentence that follows: "Then Simon Peter comes following . . . and sees the linen clothes lying."

Some ancient authorities include the following verse in Luke's Gospel that adds additional emphasis to John's description of amazement over the condition of the empty tomb: "Then arose Peter, and ran unto the sepulchre; and stooping down, he beheld the linen clothes laid by themselves, and departed, wondering in himself." (Luke 24:12) Why should the Apostle Peter leave the grave wondering? What was there about the situation to inspire awe? Plainly this question cannot be answered merely by the fact that the tomb was found empty. A deeper reason is needed to explain the impression that sent the two disciples away silent and subdued.

It would seem from John's description that there were three bewildering facts that confronted those who came to the tomb on that memorable Easter morning, facts for which they were totally unprepared:

(a) The stone which covered the mouth of the sepulchre had been rolled away and the body of Jesus was missing.

(b) The grave-clothes had not been carried away, as would have been assumed, but were left behind in the tomb.

(c) Still more mystifying, the wrappings seem to have been left behind in such a peculiar position as to indicate that the body could not possibly have been borne away by human hands. Let us consider these three aspects of the problem in their logical sequence:

When Mary Magdalene and the other women arrived at the sepulchre, doubtless bringing a liquid nard with which to anoint the face and neck of Jesus, they were totally unprepared for what they found there. Occupied by their concern over how they should move the great stone from the mouth of the tomb, they had no inkling or expectation of anything out of the ordinary. The upset came when they found the stone rolled back and the tomb empty. What could have become of the missing body? Who could have taken it away? And for what reason?

Had Nicodemus decided to remove it to some different location? Had the Jewish or Roman authorities ordered its removal? Or was it some passing marauder who had stolen it for the value of the clothing and spices with which it was embalmed? Something like these thoughts must have been surging through the minds of the women at the time; and their conviction, at first glance, seems to have been that someone had taken the body away. "Sir," said the Magdalene a few minutes later, "if thou hast borne him hence, tell me where thou hast laid him, and I will take him away."

But their upset over the empty tomb was only the first of the surprises which were to follow in rapid-fire succession on that far-off morning. The mystery deepens with every turn. When Peter and John arrive at the sepulchre, they not only find the body of Jesus missing as the women had reported;

but more puzzling still, *the grave-clothes had been left behind in the tomb.* What earthly reason could there be for removing the body of a dead man and leaving behind the wrappings with which it was embalmed? If Nicodemus, or even the enemies of Jesus, had removed the body to another location, they would certainly have carried it away in the same condition they found it. If some ordinary robber had stolen it, why did he not carry away the linen, since this would have been the only thing of value he might have desired? The presence of the grave-clothes was as inexplicable to the apostles as the fact that the tomb was empty.

Yet added to the two perplexing realities cited above, there remained a third still more mysterious problem that confronted the two men: The wrappings had not only been left behind for no apparent reason; but it would seem they had been left in such a striking position as to hold the attention of Peter and John in rapt amazement. Why did the author of the Fourth Gospel, himself the eyewitness, say concerning John, *"And he saw and believed"? Saw* what? *Believed* what? Would the mere fact that the grave-clothes had been left behind produce faith? Hardly. Instead, the two men would have thought of marauders disturbing the grave and removing the body; but not of a resurrection. Undoubtedly, Peter and John saw the position of the wrappings was such that earthly ingenuity could not possibly have removed the body without disturbing them; and this of itself made them certain that Christ had risen from the dead.

An additional aspect of the total picture confronting the disciples had to do with the spices with which the body of Jesus was embalmed. We are told that in the burial of Jesus, Nicodemus "brought a mixture of myrrh and aloes about an hundred pounds weight" and that he and those about him took the body of Jesus and "wound it in linen clothes with the spices as the manner of the Jews is to bury." Such a bulky object as a hundred pounds of spices would have been quite conspicuous. Since no mention is made of their presence in the sepulchre, one might reasonably infer that they themselves were an important part of the mystery. In fact, Chrysostom, one of the ancient Church fathers, suggests this.

In his Eighty-fifth Homily on St. John, Chrysostom describes the linen as a "sign" of the resurrection and raises the question of robbers having stolen or removed the body. He contends that no thief would have gone to the trouble of stripping the corpse before removing it, but would have taken the body as it was. "On this account," says the venerable father, "John tells us by anticipation that it was buried with much *myrrh, which glues linen to the body no less firmly than lead;* in order that thou mayst not endure those who say that it was stolen. For why should a thief undo the clothes? A thief would not have been so foolish as to spend so much trouble in a superfluous manner."

If Chrysostom is right in his observation, in order for the body to be removed and the wrappings left behind, it would have been necessary to have torn these clothes from the body strip by strip. In this case, they would have been littered about the floor of the tomb, or piled with the spices in one corner. But there seems to have been no litter, no sign of disturbance or haste. Instead of being scattered loosely on the floor, the adhering clothes had remained undisturbed in their original position to constitute a supreme, yet silent witness of Jesus' resurrection. This fact seems to be further borne out by the words in Matthew (28:6), "Come see the place where the Lord lay"; and the parallel passage in Mark (16:6), "Behold the place where they laid him." Both of these requests give the idea that there must have been something important to look at.

If the resurrection had been merely the re-animation of a corpse, as some have contended, and Jesus had simply come forth from the tomb in a physical form as did Lazarus "swathed in linen bands," then the discarded clothing would be wholly unexplainable. It would have been necessary for Jesus to wear them until more suitable coverings could have been found. Why should he leave them behind when they might be used, and necessarily must be used, if he left the tomb in any but a naked condition? On the other hand, if the Master, by some strange metamorphosis as yet only faintly comprehended, had assumed a purely spiritual existence, then the leaving behind of the linen needs no explanation; for with the assumption of his "pneumatic" body, material coverings were no longer of further service.

We are startled to hear of matter vanishing away, passing from sight and touch with no residium left; yet puzzling as are the events revealed in the resurrection stories, their genuine historic character is receiving new support at the present time from a number of developments in important areas of exploration. Two challenging facts have emerged that have radically altered the old materialistic position of physical science and have tended to diminish, or perhaps even remove, the chief obstacle which prevents the claims of the Christian religion from being taken seriously. The first of these is the modern dynamic theory of matter; and the second is the extensive work now being done in psychical research.

Ours is the first age in which there is no such thing as dead matter. Heretofore the real has been identified as the concrete; but mechanistic materialism has now given way to nuclear physics with its mystic atom which is regarded as being as porous as the solar system. Sir Arthur Eddington says that if all space were removed from the atoms which compose the body of the largest man, it would constitute a speck barely visible to the most powerful microscope. The brilliant astronomer, Sir James Jeans, has suggested that we may eventually discover that substance is our greatest illusion and that reality is wholly mental. "The stream of knowledge," says he, "is heading toward a non-material reality; the universe begins to look more like a great thought than like a great machine."

We have long been told by those who claim to know that the human body is in a continuous state of transformation, making and unmaking itself through the creation and destruction of tissue and bone structure, until at the end of seven years, every particle of the original body has been burned up or destroyed and a new body created. Thus a man of fifty has worn out seven bodies and is beginning on his eighth. When viewed in this light, the vanishing away of the material particles which composed the physical body of Jesus does not seem any more mysterious than the vanishing away of other human bodies; aside from the fact that in the former instance the time element was speeded up.

Since physical science has now become transcendental, it is entirely possible that the metaphysics of tomorrow may turn out to be nearer that of the first century than the twentieth. While the religionist must not expect too much at this point, yet the positive gain for religion is evident. Because of this change of front on the part of the physical sciences, there is being made possible an intellectual atmosphere in which the ancient truths of Christianity may be recognized and accepted as truths.

A significant aspect of this new concept of the physical universe is that at precisely the same moment in history when the nuclear scientists have come to regard matter as simply "frozen" energy and not as the impenetrable solid it was once thought to be, the psychological laboratories have yielded new evidence for the reality of a supersensible order of things. Throughout the world today, there is a small but highly competent number of individuals and groups who are exploring the area of extrasensory perception and other metaphysical forces in much the same way as atomic scientists are studying the atom, and with astonishing results.

Few persons are aware of the careful and extensive work that has been done during the past three-quarters of a century, and particularly the past two decades, in the field of psychical research. While psychic manifestation is as old as the race, man's attempt to study it systematically is of comparatively recent origin. The first serious attempt to investigate it had its beginning in England in 1882 with the formation of the British Society for Psychical Research by a group of Cambridge scholars. Its first president was Professor Henry Sidgwick, then the most influential man at Cambridge, with Dr. Edmund Gurney and the author and poet, Frederic W. H. Myers, as the original organizers of the group. They were later joined in their quest by a number of other outstanding individuals, including the noted physicist Sir **William Barrett, Professor J. J. Thomson, the eminent** biologist, Alfred Russell Wallace, Sir Oliver Lodge, and William E. Gladstone, the Prime Minister of Great Britain who estimated the work of the society as "the most important work being done in the world—by far the most important."

The moving spirit of this early group was Myers, who was passionately devoted to discovering the truth of human survival, being determined to spend his life's energy "beating against the walls of the prisonhouse in case a panel anywhere might yield." In his monumental work, *Human Personality and its Survival of Bodily Death*, which has become a classic in its field, he urged that the time is ripe for "a study of unseen things as strenuous as that which science has made familiar for the problems of earth."

Two years later a similar group was organized in America that numbered among its early supporters Professor William James of Harvard and Dr. James Hyslop, who resigned his professorship at Columbia University to become its full-time secretary. These men approached their task in a strictly scientific and objective manner and could have taken as their motto the words of Louis Pasteur: "In all this there is no question of religion, nor philosophy, nor atheism, nor materialism, nor spiritualism, it is entirely a question of fact." The work of these societies now covers over eighty years of research and investigation and constitutes a veritable mine of carefully documented evidence of high significance.

Up to the present, the majority of academically trained people have given little or no serious attention to the work being done in psychical research. Its ideas have not confronted them as meaningful and revolutionary for their whole philosophy of life; yet its findings promise to have far-reaching effects upon the future religious outlook.

Professor A. C. Hardy, England's most eminent biologist, felt that the work now being done in this field of investigation may eventually reconcile science and religion. In his Essex Hall lecture he said: "If only one percent of the money spent on the physical and biological sciences could be spent on the investigation of religious experience and psychical research, it might not be long before a new age of faith had dawned upon the world. It would, I believe, be a faith in a spiritual reality to match that of the Middle Ages; one based not upon a miraculous interference with the source of nature, but upon a greatly widened scientific outlook."

Among a number of important effects of psychical research is that it is furnishing strong and additional evidence in support of three basic Christian claims:

(a) It has demonstrated the non-physical nature of man and the reality of a supersensuous world.

(b) It has furnished new and additional insight into the nature and reality of the resurrection of Jesus Christ.

(c) It has made the Christian belief in life after death an almost practical certainty based on empirical and scientific evidence not heretofore possible.

The first of these results is that psychic research is furnishing irrefutable evidence to support the Christian position that man has an ultimate dimension of being and is built on the scale of two worlds, not one. The ancient Greek idea that nothing gets into the mind except by way of the senses has been disproved by the discovery of "a new frontier of the mind" which gives hints of the larger nature of man.

Sir George Thomson, professor of physics at the Imperial College of Sciences, who was awarded the Nobel Prize for Physics in 1937, expressed his views upon the subject in *The Sunday Times* of London, December 7, 1937, when he stated that the evidence for telepathy, clairvoyance, and other psychokinetic forces is so strong that their general acceptance is prevented only by the fact that they upset orthodox notions. Professor Robert H. Thouless of Cambridge University, who has made extensive studies in the field and who contributed the article on "Psychic Research" to the current issue of *The Encyclopedia Britannica* said essentially the same thing when he wrote in 1942, "The reality of the phenomena must be regarded as proved as certainly as anything in scientific research can be proved."

A mass of factual data is emerging so extensive as to convince many well known scientists and philosophers that the materialistic view of man has been experimentally refuted. A person standing by a mechanically operated dice-throwing machine in the parapsychology department of Duke University and wishing for a certain result has affected the roll of the dice. Nelya Mikhailova, a Russian housewife living on the edge of Leningrad, has displayed a new and unknown form of energy. By simply concentrating on certain objects, she is able to move and control them. Under her influence, compasses have been made to spin, the pendulum of a wall clock has been stopped, and scattered matches or a fountain pen made to move across the table towards her or away from her. A psychic force released from the subliminal mind of Ted Serios, a Chicago truck driver, affects the emulsion on photographic film. By staring into the lens of an ordinary camera and "willing" a picture to come, Serios has produced, under stringent test conditions, inexplicable photographs by thought photography. These and other remarkable things, both spontaneous as well as experimental, are now taking place throughout the world that would suggest a massive breakthrough into a new realm of reality.

A second contribution of psychical research is that it has thrown new light upon the nature and reality of Jesus' risen body; and has given additional weight to the Christian claims of his historic resurrection. A physical form elastic enough to be touched and handled on one occasion and yet of such a non-physical nature as to appear or vanish through closed doors, certainly does not fit into the materialistic dogmas of the past. Yet the work of certain experimentalists indicates that there are unknown forces in the human organism that are capable of being externalized and projected outwardly in ectoplasmic, phantasmal, and telekinetic forms that seem startingly similar to the accounts in the four gospels of the Soma Pheumatikon, or risen body of Jesus.

The distinguished chemist and physicist, Sir William Crookes, whose discovery and magnetic bending of the cathode-ray laid the foundations of electronics and prepared the way for nuclear fission, spent many years of his life studying psychic forces and was the first man in modern times whose investigations gave him a glimpse of other states of matter than were recorded by traditional physics. He began his investigations believing the whole affair was superstition and trickery and that the scientific methods which he would apply would drive "the worthless residuum into the limbo of magic and necromancy." He ended up by staking his scientific reputation on the fact that his preconceived ideas were wrong and that a class of phenomena wholly new to science did really exist.

The attitude of the scientific world towards Crookes at the time was characteristic and contemptible. When some of his colleagues heard that he was beginning his investigations they said, "Now that a real scientist is on the track, the fraud will soon be exposed." But when he completed his study and felt compelled by the evidence to accept the fact of metaphysical realities they said, "Poor old fellow, he has evidently gone off his head!" Crookes was elected President of the Royal Academy of Science but was later dropped because he refused to give up his studies in psychical research, the lesser scientists apparently feeling they would be stigmatized by his interests if he were not in some way condemned. Ten years later, however, he was re-elected as President of the Academy because he was unquestionably Britain's greatest scientist at the time.

At his second inauguration in Albert Memorial Hall in

London he told the world that his attitude toward the paranormal had not changed and said: "There are many here tonight who believe that one reason I have been re-elected president is because I have abandoned my studies in the field of psychical phenomena. They should know that during the past ten years I have continued these studies and am more convinced than ever of the significance and importance of the facts discovered in this field."

Later Crookes summed up the result of his research into materializations, ectoplasm, levitations, and other psychic forces by saying: "I have both seen and heard, in a manner which would make unbelief impossible, things called spiritual, which cannot be taken by a rational being to be capable of explanation by imposture, coincidence, or mistake . . . . I do not say such things are possible, I say they exist."

Although Crookes was the first leading man of science who undertook to test metaphysical realities by modern experimental techniques, he was followed by a number of distinguished researchers who continued the work: Dr. Charles Richet, professor of psychology at the University of Paris; Italy's Cesare Lombroso, psychiatrist and criminologist; physicist Sir Oliver Lodge; Professor and Madame Curie, the discoverers of radium; Munich's Albert Baron von Schrenck-Notzing, a physician noted for his pioneering use of hypnosis; Hans Driesch, professor of philosophy at Leipzig; Gustave Geley, who abandoned his medical practice to become director of the Institut Metapsychique International in Paris; and others of similar stature.

All of these persons made extensive studies in the field over a number of years and reached strikingly similar conclusions as to the reality of what they found. The work of Richet—himself a Nobel Prize winner and the author of *Thirty Years of Psychic Research*—might be taken as illustrative of the scope and nature of the results attained by the entire group. In the introduction to his book, he gives this significant evaluation of the findings: "In spite of the great advance in physics, chemistry, and physiology, the laws of these sciences, as at present known, do not account for certain exceptional phenomena, and these phenomena being inexplicable by orthodox science, it has been found convenient to ignore . . . . Nevertheless the facts are facts; they are numerous, authentic, and startling."

Richet then sums up the results of his work by declaring that the following truths "have been placed beyond doubt": (a) the reality of cryptesthesia—the human mind has sources of cognition that disclose facts which neither sight, hearing, nor touch could reveal; and (b) the reality of ectoplasms or materialisms—there are powers emerging from the human body that can take form and act as if they were material bodies. Concerning the latter he writes:

The fact that intelligent forces are projected from an organism, that can act mechanically, can move objects and make sounds, is a phenomenon as certainly established as any facts in physics . . . . I shall not waste time in stating the absurdities, almost the impossibilities, from a psycho-physiological point of view, of this phenomenon . . . . I say that under certain exceptional conditions—and I admit that the conditions are extremely exceptional—the semblance of a living hand is formed which has all the properties of a living hand and seems to belong to a being similar to a human being! . . . This is surely the climax of marvels! *Nevertheless it is a fact.*

Some of the best documented work in the paranormal field at the present time is being done in Germany under the direction of Professor Hans Bender, M.D., Ph.D., a psychiatrist who directs a team of researchers at the Institute for Border Areas of Psychology and Mental Health at Freiburg University and has established a reputation as Germany's foremost parapsychologist. Dr. Bender reports dealing with numerous astonishing cases of psycho-kinesis—the movement of physical objects by some unknown mind-directed energy —the phenomena of levitation and teleportation, and other physical demonstrations of psychic activities, now coming to be called, "recurrent spontaneous psycho-kinesis." One of the most startling of these physical manifestations reported by Bender is that of "apports," by which is meant the transportation of a material object from one place to another, involving as it does the penetration of matter through matter, such as would be necessary in the case of the appearance or disappearance of objects from closed and sealed rooms.

Such happenings as these, vouched for by men of the integrity and competence of Crookes, Richet and Bender, are as startling and arresting as they are inexplicable; yet there is a striking similarity between the phenomena they described and what we read about in the gospel records of the resurrection. The accounts of the de-materialization of Jesus' earthly body inside the tomb, his passing out of the encompassing grave-clothes without disturbing them, and the re-materialization of his personal form in the presence of his disciples are analogous to much of what makes up the factual data of contemporary metaphysical research.

While the New Testament writers make it plain that what took place surrounding the resurrection of Jesus was something far more august and authoritative than mere phenomenalism, yet the two classes of events have many qualities in common and would seem to be of essentially the same character. The fact that the resurrection stories have their contemporary counterparts in much that is being brought to light by experimental science today is an encouraging development that can have significance for the future of religion.

Due to the materialistic agnosticism that followed in the wake of Darwin's evolutionary theory, the poet Frederic W. H. Myers was swept away from the moorings of established religion and was only restored to a religious faith through the results of his extended investigations of metaphysical realities. At the turn of the century, he made the bold prophecy that the result of such efforts would ultimately re-establish belief in the gospel record of the rising of Christ from the dead; and that "in consequence of the new psychic evidence, all reasonable men, a century hence, will believe the resurrection of Christ, whereas, in default of the new evidence no reasonable man, a century hence, would have believed it."

Perhaps Myers overstated the case, since almost three-quarters of a century has gone by and it is still true that more people believe *without* the material evidence he spoke of than those who do. However, this is not to imply that such evidence is without real significance. As a result of it, many people are now gaining new insight into the real nature of Jesus' resurrection and new confidence in the integrity of the gospel records that bear witness to it.

A third contribution of psychical research is that it has furnished convincing evidence for the fact of man's survival of death. A basis for the belief in the continuity of human existence has now been established on other than religious grounds. Belief in human survival no longer rests solely upon traditional or subjective reasons heretofore advanced but upon objective and scientific proof as well. This is a highly important development.

A considerable segment of present-day Christians have only a weak and tenuous belief in life after death. This is illustrated by the results of a Gallup poll taken a few years ago in England from a representative cross section of regular churchgoers, 33 percent of whom had no conviction of another life. Another 33 percent did not know or hadn't thought anything about it, and only 34 percent of the regular churchgoers really believed in life after death. Many Christian clergymen in their preaching have nothing to offer their congregations concerning the fact of death and the future life except broad generalizations and vague hopes. In spite of the fact that Jesus himself was as certain of the reality of the future life as he was that the wind blew or the sun shone, the belief of many of these men called to represent him is honeycombed with doubt and misgivings. One of them remarked, "When it comes to immortality I think all gray. I don't know what I believe."

The reality of life after death has now become established as an almost practical certainty by positive evidence of an empirical nature. Of course this statement will be open to question. Extreme skepticism inevitably greets every purported proof of human survival. There is a sort of scientific superstition to the effect that proof of it is incapable of demonstration by any set of objective facts or observations whatsoever that mankind can make. This resolutely agnostic view is almost universally held at the present time by those who are unaware of the available evidence to the contrary.

Christian spokesmen, including public speakers and writers, have easily accepted the above dictum as true, and with unfailing regularity they go on reminding us that it is impossible to prove that a man goes on living after death. Muddle-minded preachers, with false Christian modesty, join in cooing the same negative refrain in spite of the incontrovertible fact that the loftiest and purest minds of the race—even non-Christians such as Socrates and Plato—from time immemorial have held to the truth of man's immortality; that Jesus himself accepted the reality of the future life as the background assumption of all he did and said; and that his resurrection was a tangible demonstration of the truth that human personality does survive the grave.

However, those who have taken the time and the trouble to study the facts for themselves dispute the negative dogma. There is a growing mass of sifted evidence pointing in the direction of survival after death whose cumulative effect is highly impressive. Some of the most distinguished persons in science and philosophy, who have spent the major part of their life's energy probing the evidence, have reached the conclusion that survival has been demonstrated by positive proof. To be sure, it is not the same type of proof as that produced in a chemical laboratory; but neither is an eclipse of the sun, a thunderstorm, or proof of human love between man and wife arrived at by the test-tube variety of evidence which can be created or controlled at will. Nor can even the most perfect proof be always guaranteed to inevitably convince everyone.

Truth is never coercive; and it is possible to deny any known fact, including the most universally accepted truths of modern science and observation. An example of this is the presence in our midst of the Flat Earth Society, composed of people who still remain unconvinced as to the rotundity of the earth. Since absolute proof of anything is rarely possible, and any fact may be doubted or denied, the highest kind of certainty one need ever expect to obtain in this world is that which excludes reasonable doubt. It is this kind of proof of human survival which, according to these men, has now been attained.

Robert Crookall, Ph.D., a retired geologist living in England who has written a number of books on astral projection, estimates that of those who have studied the direct evidence for survival over a period of years and published an account of their quest, 81 percent became absolutely sure of survival on evidential grounds, 14 percent were more or less convinced, while 5 percent remained more or less doubtful. Some of them, such as Dr. Richard Hodgson of Cambridge, Alfred Russell Wallace, co-discoverer with Darwin of the law of natural selection, and Professor Raoul Pictet of the University of Genoa, began their investigations profoundly skeptical, not believing in life after death, but after years of study became convinced of it by the sheer weight of evidence.

A typical example of this sort was that of Dr. James Hyslop, Professor of Logic and Ethics at Columbia University. Hyslop was so profoundly skeptical of life after death that his skepticism became a matter of public comment. In his early years of teaching in the Department of Philosophy at Columbia, he lectured to students of the various theological schools in and around New York City who were taking courses in philosophy in order to qualify themselves for higher degrees. Some of the contemporary theologians and ministers protested against Hyslop because they felt that he was too skeptical to teach men who were devoting their lives to the Christian ministry. An anonymous round-robin protest was directed against him in an attempt to get him ousted from his position. Later, Hyslop began a study of psychic phenomena and, after years of intensive investigation in the field, reached a position of such certainty concerning human survival as to declare:

> I regard the evidence of survival after death conclusive. ...Telepathy is not a legitimate rival.... It has been eliminated for all who know anything about the facts and is pressed only by those who are too bewildered by the phenomena to make up their minds....There is no other rational explanation of the facts than the hypothesis of survival; and the cumulative evidence is so strong that I do not hesitate to say that the proof is even equal or superior to that of evolution.

The great French astronomer, Dr. Camille Flammarion, a member of the French Academy of Science, investigated paranormal phenomena for over sixty years and produced ten books on the subject. His three volumes on *Death and Its Mystery* is the largest collection of case studies in this field that has yet been published. In the concluding chapter of this massive work, he sums up the results of his years of study in the following unequivocal statement: "The object of this work has been attained.... From this time on we may be certain—and our certainty is based on scientific proof—that the soul survives after the last earthly breath has been drawn. *The soul is independent of the material organism and continues to live on after death.*"

A more contemporary example is that of Dr. William McDougall, one of the most respected of modern psychologists who, although one of the most conservative of investigators in the realm of parapsychology, concluded that the evidence at hand indicated either survival, or telepathy "of the most far-reaching and improbable sort." Dr. Raynor C. Johnson, Master of Queen's College in the University of Melbourne, Australia, himself a physicist of note, says essentially the same thing in his valuable book, *The Imprisoned Splendor.* He sums up his findings by asserting that the data of psychical research lead him to conclude that there is a personal life independent of the physical body; and that "if survival of death is not rigorously proven, it is nevertheless established as that higher order of probability which, for practical purposes, can be taken as the same thing."

Dr. Nador Fodor, the distinguished Hungarian psychoanalyst who was for some time Director of the International Institute for Psychical Research, London, and who published *The Encyclopedia of Psychic Science*, reached a similar position; as did the late Dr. Hornell Hart, Professor of Sociology and Anthropology at Florida Southern College. Dr. Hart, who achieved international reputation based on his quarter century investigation of ESP Project, closes his important book, *The Enigma of Survival*, with this clear-cut and positive affirmation: "Human personality *does* survive death. This is the outcome which I found emerging when the strongest anti-survivalist arguments and the rebuttals are considered thoroughly, with dispassionate open-mindedness."

It is evident that the testimonies of the above experimentalists to a belief in life after death are not the hasty opinions of uninformed minds but are the deliberate judgments of highly qualified men, trained in the techniques of science and capable of sifting evidence. Such men have spent years of their lives investigating the truth of the facts for which they vouch. They not only personally believed in the reality of human survival, but they held that there is ample and conclusive proof of the fact.

Added to numerous examples of exploration in the *Psi* field of a laboratory type, there are significant cases of individuals who have made substantial contributions to the field of extrasensory evidence through investigating phenomena which developed in their own homes and with members of their own families. Two cases of this sort may be mentioned.

The first is that of Dr. Horace Westwood, a Unitarian minister, whose daughter manifested extrasensory powers of a high order at the age of eleven and was the vehicle of carefully arranged tests over a period of several years and the subject of his extraordinary book, *There Is a Psychic World.* Oddly enough, even though a Christian minister, Westwood held a naturalistic outlook and did not believe in, or even desire, a life after death. However, his outlook was so revolutionized by the spontaneous occurrences which took place in his own home that, even against his will, he became convinced of the reality of human survival.

A second, and even better known, example is that of the novelist and distinguished writer, Stewart Edward White, the story of whose experimental work with his spiritually sensitive wife, Betty, over a period of twenty years and her subsequent death is embodied in what is now generally agreed to be three of the most significant books yet written dealing with life after death—*The Betty Book, Across the Unknown,* and *The Unobstructed Universe.* Booth Tarkington declared the last-named to be "the most important book ever written on the most important of all subjects." No publication has been made of the fact that a number of unidentified scientists have clandestinely derived important clews from it for their work in nuclear experimentation.

There are encouraging effects of this new outlook in the lives of numerous individuals at the present time. With some it is producing conviction of the life ahead never before felt; for others who already believe, it is giving additional reasons for so doing. Dr. Ralph Harlow, who spent many years personally investigating metaphysical realities and whose book, *A Life After Death,* is one of the most enlightening and valuable in the field, once remarked: "I do not believe in immortality because of my psychic experience, nor of my study in the field. I believe in it because of the kind of God I have experienced in my life and what I have found of him in Jesus Christ; yet my experience of the psychic has greatly increased my faith."

A few years before his death, Sherwood Eddy, the well known author and missionary leader, expressed to the writer his confidence in the certainty of the life ahead in a clear-cut and memorable declaration. He said: "I now believe in personal immortality, not only on the grounds of faith, but because of empirical evidence from years of psychic experience and psychic investigation. My experience of it has been so repeated, so convincing and so satisfying to me personally that I now have the same evidence in principle for the existence of the seven members of my family who are now in the unobstructed universe that I have for the five members of my family who are still on earth. My belief in personal immortality was once a matter of faith; now it is faith *plus* knowledge."

Because of the new evidence opening up, the belief of an increasing number of people now no longer rests solely upon their Christian faith but, like my friend's, upon faith plus empirical knowledge. This is an encouraging development. The early Church utilized psychic events as literal testimony and persuasion. The dawn of Christianity was associated with psychic happenings on an unprecedented scale. The thing that gave primitive Christianity its hold over men's minds was that it was a religion of spirit and power. Paul's conversion experience on the road to Damascus, the clairvoyant vision of Stephen at his stoning, the tongues of fire and the rushing wind on the day of Pentecost, the "signs and wonders" wrought by the hands of the apostles, Peter's release from prison at the hand of a spirit-guide—these and scores of other examples might be cited to show how closely the spirit-life impinged upon the early Christians and gave to the new movement its power and vitality. It is quite evident that if such things had been deleted from the experience of the early church, primitive Christianity would have been left barren indeed.

Jesus himself did not discount the necessity and value of sensory knowledge in creating faith, He recognized its rudimentary importance. When Thomas demanded physical proof of the resurrection, Jesus gave him the opportunity of touching the crucifixion wounds; for Jesus knew that unless the mind is convinced there can be no peace of soul. It was the material evidence that confronted Peter and John at the open tomb on Easter morning that gave them their certainty that Jesus had risen. They *saw* the linen clothes *and believed.* It should be remembered, however, that what they saw at that time was but a part of a much larger body of evidence that had been given them previously. In fact, their visit to the sepulchre was but the culmination of a series of physical events in the life of Jesus which, in many ways, were as puzzling and difficult to explain as was the enigma of the empty tomb itself.

There had been foreshadowings of an illusive and astral quality about Jesus' body even during his public ministry. On a number of occasions, it seemed to possess powers and obey higher laws than those to which ordinary humanity was subject. These qualities were of such a striking and extraordinary nature as to suggest to King Herod the possibility of one having risen from the dead. Two of the best attested incidents in the cycle of gospel tradition—the walking on the Sea of Galilee and the Transfiguration—are examples of this. The first was a kind of levitation that countered gravity, and the second was a momentary release of hidden inner powers. Both of these manifestations were hints or gleams of slumbering potentialities that were later to be manifested in Jesus in an even more striking form.

There is a very definite connection between what the two apostles encountered at the sepulchre and the momentary metamorphosis of Jesus which took place on a mountain a short time before the crucifixion. In this dramatic event, we are told that during a period of high spiritual communion the physical form of Jesus became changed to an intense luminosity on the order of molten steel, a curious detail of which was that this "shining whiteness" affected his clothes as well as his body. This experience is told by all three of the synoptic writers but appears in its oldest form in Mark 9:2-10 where we read:

And after six days Jesus took with him Peter and James and John, and led them up a high mountain apart by themselves; and he was transfigured before them, and his garments became glistening, intensely white, as no fuller on earth could bleach them. And there appeared to them Elijah with Moses; and they were talking to Jesus. And Peter said to Jesus, "Master, it is well that we are here; let us make three booths, one for you and one for Moses and one for Elijah." For he did not know what to say, for they were exceedingly afraid. And a cloud overshadowed them, and a voice came out of the cloud, "This is my beloved Son; listen to him." And suddenly looking around they no longer saw anyone with them but Jesus only. And as they were coming down the mountain, he charged them to tell no one what they had seen, until the Son of Man should have risen from the dead. So they kept the matter to themselves, questioning what the rising from the dead meant.

Difficult as it may be for moderns to accept as literal happenings an account of clothes turning white as light, hearing a voice speaking from the skies, or having persons long since dead become visible, there does not seem to be any alternative but to regard the story of the Transfiguration as a simple and direct description of an actual event in the life of Jesus—something that left a profound and lasting impression upon the three men who shared the wonder of the hour with him. The incident fits logically into the sequence of events of Jesus' life and has a definite connection with the things that followed later.

That Jesus had gone up on the mountain for prayer and spiritual renewal in preparation for the ordeal of the cross is indicated by the fact that the topic of conversation between him and the two patriarchs was "his decease which he should accomplish at Jerusalem." An additional end the experience served was that of preparing the three disciples for ultimately accepting the truth of the resurrection by giving them a glimpse of things to come. The author of The Apocalypse of Peter brings this out when he says, "Our Lord showed at the Transfiguration the apparel of the last days, of the day of resurrection, unto Peter, and James, and John." Because they had seen the body of Jesus momentarily transformed, they were able to grasp the possibility of their Master appearing to them later in a form somewhat different from what they had known previously and yet be certain that it was he.

Without the resurrection which followed, the incident on the mountain would appear somewhat meaningless; but place the two events side by side, and immediately we see a connection between them, the former helping to explain the latter by familiarizing the disciples with the idea of existence in a disembodied or altered form. In the account of the visit of Peter and John at the sepulchre, the narrative makes us feel that the two apostles never for a moment supposed that human hands had borne the body away. What they saw there called back their experience at the Transfiguration and also the words of the Master as they came down the mountain. He had charged them at the time to "tell no man [apparently not even the other disciples] the things they had seen until the Son of Man should be raised from the dead." The request had puzzled them and they wondered "what the rising from the dead could mean." Later, however, as they pondered the significance of the empty grave-clothes, the meaning of the request became clear. The idea of the metamorphosis of Jesus' body took hold upon them and they became certain that the resurrection had taken place because they saw the essential similarity between the two events.

It has been suggested that the riddle of the empty grave-wrappings became an open "sign" to the general public that helped to break up the ground for the apostles' preaching and to explain the immediate phenomenal success of the early Christian movement. This would seem to be the case, since early Christian writings indicate that the open tomb became an immediate object of public interest. In fact, the apocryphal Gospel of Peter, written in the second century, tells how "there came a great multitude from Jerusalem and the region round about to see the sepulchre that had been sealed."

It is reasonable to infer that the throngs which came out to visit the tomb were so impressed by what they saw there that in succeeding days they became susceptible to the preaching of the resurrection because they themselves had seen a visible proof of its actuality. Thus the first inkling of the resurrection truth was given to the world by the phenomenon of the undisturbed grave-clothes. It was their mute but impressive testimony, interpreted by the disciples' previous experience of the Transfiguration, that sent Peter and John on that far-off morning silent from the tomb with the dawning conviction that the gates of Death had been broken and "the Man of Mystery had gone his way."

CHAPTER FIVE

THE GREAT FORTY DAYS

The phenomenon of the empty grave-clothes was the material evidence that first alerted the minds of Peter and John to the possibility of a resurrection; but it was the post-crucifixion appearances of Jesus that authenticated its reality and created the Easter Faith. On this point the records are unmistakable. All the four gospels, Acts, and the letters of Paul bring out the fact that following his death Christ returned to his disciples as one alive from the dead; coming to them from time to time, holding conversation with them, and, according to Luke's account, even eating with them before he finally went away and his visible manifestations ceased. It was these awesome and authoritative visits that convinced the first apostles of the truth of Jesus' resurrection and sent eager and excited men to the confines of the Roman Empire to tell the story.

The events that are recorded as having taken place during the period of the Great Forty Days are without parallel in literature and outweigh in interest and significance any other series of facts known to man. It is difficult to work out a consistent chronology for these separate appearances, for the gospels themselves differ in certain matters of detail and a complete harmony cannot be established at all points among them. In this they would seem to conform to normal human experience. It is quite rare for two or more independent accounts of the same event, although written in good faith, to achieve a perfect unanimity. When confronted with these differences in the resurrection stories, a dear friend once replied, "Aren't you glad it is that way?" Her meaning was easily caught. She was simply rejoicing in the natural human differences found in them, which to her, and to others, give evidence of the fact that the records are not a "frame-up." Had the narratives been identical in every respect, it might have suggested collusion on the part of the writers and seriously impaired the essential value of their witness.

It is necessary to remember that the various accounts represent happenings to a number of people at different times and places and under a variety of circumstances. It is evident that only a small part of what Jesus did and said during this memorable period has come down to us. In fact, the author of the Fourth Gospel definitely states as much when he says, "Many other signs did Jesus in the presence of his disciples which are not written in this book." Of the recorded visits which took place during this interval of six weeks some have a few descriptive details; while others are merely mentioned without giving us any of the circumstances surrounding them.

There are two such meetings of first-rate importance to the early church which carry no details. One of them was to James, the Lord's brother, who later became head of the church at Jerusalem and whom the Jewish historian Josephus mentions as having met his death by martyrdom in the year 62 A.D. During the earthly ministry of Jesus we know almost nothing of him. The evidence seems conclusive that he was not one of Jesus' followers at that time, but was indifferent, or even hostile, to his Brother's mission until after the resurrection.

James' conversion to the faith, from many standpoints, was as unexpected and remarkable as that of the Apostle Paul. We know nothing of the circumstantial influences that brought him into the camp of the Christians; but a single reference in the letters of Paul gives us the hard-core reason. In summarizing the main facts of his gospel to the church at Corinth, the great Apostle writes:

I passed on to you what I received, which is of the greatest importance: that Christ died for our sins, as written in the Scriptures; that he was buried and raised to life on the third day, as written in the Scriptures; that he appeared to Peter, and then to all twelve apostles. Then he appeared to more than five hundred of his followers at once, most of whom are still alive, although some have died. Then he appeared to James, and then to all the apostles. Last of all he appeared to me. (I Cor. 15:3-8)

However much we might wish to know the intriguing details of this significant encounter of Jesus with a man who at first was skeptical and antagonistic to his leadership but who later became the dominant figure in the Jerusalem church, aside from this single reference, the New Testament is silent upon the matter. However, in an old apocryphal book called The Gospel of Hebrews, of which only a few sentences have been preserved, there is a curious fragment describing how Jesus appeared to his brother James, which may embody a genuine historical reminiscence:

Now the Lord, when he had given the linen cloth unto the servant of the priest, went unto James and appeared to him (for James had sworn that he would not eat bread from that hour wherein he had drunk the Lord's cup until he should see him risen again from among them that sleep), and again after a little, "Bring ye, saith the Lord, a table and bread," and immediately it is added, "He took bread and blessed and brake it and gave it unto James the Just and said unto him, My brother, eat thy bread, for the Son of Man is risen from among them that sleep."

This passage might imply that James was present at the Last Supper, or it may have some other reference; but at any rate, it adds point to the fact that it was the resurrection that changed him from an erstwhile doubter and antagonist of

Jesus into one of the most powerful leaders of the early Christian movement. It is said that Christians inscribed upon his monument the words: "He hath been a true witness both to the Jews and to the Greeks that Jesus is Christ."

Another appearance to a member of the apostolic group of high import for the primitive church, but of which we have no details, was that to Simon Peter. There are two meager references to this meeting. The first of these is carried in Paul's list to the Corinthian church; and the second in Luke's description of the Emmaus incident that took place in the late afternoon of Easter Day. It will be recalled that Jesus walked the Emmaus road unrecognized by Cleopas and his companion until they reached the inn and, as the three sat at meat together, Jesus blest and broke the bread and as he did so vanished from their sight. The two disciples immediately recognized the identity of their Host; and in the excitement of the moment set out at once on their five- or six-mile journey back to Jerusalem to inform the main body of believers what had happened. On their arrival in Jerusalem, Luke related that "they found the eleven gathered together and those who were with them, who said, 'The Lord has risen indeed, and has appeared to Simon!' " (Luke 24:33)

The chronology of events would suggest that this appearance to Peter must have taken place at some time between the early morning hour when Jesus met the women at the tomb and the late afternoon of the same day when the Emmaus episode occurred. The importance of the meeting had to do with Peter's restoration. Following his denial of the Master on the eve of the crucifixion, Peter was plunged into the depths of bitter humiliation and despair. It was of prime importance to the Christian community, of which he was spokesman, that he be spiritually rehabilitated and restored to his apostleship. The significant words given in the early morning hours to the women at the tomb were, "Go tell my disciples *and Peter* that I am risen." It was this personal message, relayed by the women, that brought the first ray of hope to the humiliated and broken-hearted Apostle. But it was the encounter with Jesus himself in the afternoon that changed the unstable and vacillating disciple into the Man of Rock who ultimately was to seal his allegiance to the Christian cause by his death at Rome.

It is significant that in each of the resurrection stories where details are given, Jesus is described as entering into some sort of relationship with his friends other than merely a visionary glimpse or a flash upon the outer or inner eye. This fact is very noticeable in Jesus' first appearance to the whole apostolic company on Easter evening. In the absence of Thomas, ten of the apostles and certain others of their company were gathered in the Upper Room that tradition has commonly assumed to be "the home of Mary the mother of Mark" where the Last Supper was eaten. The doors were closed and barred lest at any moment guards from the Jewish or Roman authorities might come to arrest them as they had arrested Jesus.

A short time previous to this, Peter had rejoined the group and had reported to them the story of his meeting with Jesus in the late afternoon. The group was still breathless with excitement over the news he had brought, when Cleopas and his companion broke in upon them with their amazing tale of the Stranger who had appeared to them as they had journeyed along the road to Emmaus. The two late arrivals had barely finished their story when the Subject of their conversation himself showed up. Without warning of any kind, suddenly Jesus appeared in their midst; and at this, pandemonium almost broke out. The account says, "They were terrified and affrighted." There had been no previous indication of his coming, such as the sound of footsteps or a knock at the door. The record simply states that he "stood" in their midst. At this point Luke continues the narrative:

And while they were still talking about these things, Jesus himself stood among them and said, "Peace be to you all!" But they shrank back in terror, for they thought they were seeing a ghost. "Why are you so worried?" said Jesus, "and why do doubts arise in your minds? Look at my hands and my feet—it is really I myself! Feel me and see; ghosts have no flesh or bones as you can see that I have." But while they still could not believe it through sheer joy, and were quite bewildered, Jesus said to them, "Have you anything here to eat?" They gave him a piece of broiled fish and part of a honeycomb, which he took and ate before their eyes. (24:36-43)

It has already been observed that in the resurrection stories, Jesus appeared to his friends in a number of different forms, depending upon the circumstances of the occasion. He came to Mary in Joseph's garden in the guise of a gardener whom she thought to be the keeper of the place. Later he appeared to the seven as they fished on the Sea of Galilee and they mistook him for a strolling fisherman. In the case of the Emmaus disciples, his coming did not seem to occasion any surprise; they merely accepted him as a casual traveler journeying along the road in a pilgrim's garb. Seemingly there was nothing exceptional about the newcomer's appearance, nor did he give any evidence that his hands had been maimed or that he had been crippled in the feet. But this first visit with the ten was significantly different. He came to them as the Crucified One with pierced brow and wounds in his hands and feet; and the thing struck them with terror. As they had seen him on the cross, so was he now; and they were unprepared for such an apparition. To calm their fears, he let them examine his hands and feet and the visible marks of the crucifixion were upon them.

However, even more than the sight of his mutilated form, the thing that startled the group was the unorthodox manner of his entry unto them. How had he got in? No one had heard his coming or had opened the door to admit him. As far as we know he might have risen through the floor as easily as to have come through closed doors. It was this mysterious manner of his entry that made them think he was a spirit. A man who had been miraculously resurrected and restored to life, who had come back to them in a physical form like themselves, knocked at their door and been admitted in the usual manner, would have inspired them with surprise and gladness but would hardly have "terrified" them. His manner of coming to them did not make sense; and for this reason, it was necessary for Jesus to reassure them and convince them of his identity.

The difficulty of the ten on this occasion was the thing that Thomas later questioned. When the group told him of Jesus' coming to them, Thomas did not doubt that they had seen a ghost-like apparition; what he doubted was that this shadow they had seen had any real connection with the human Jesus. On this account, it was necessary for Jesus to convince them that he was no disembodied ghost, or an illusion of their minds. In order to add additional weight to the evidence, he asked for food. When they brought him the fish, he ate it before them; and in this homely and unpretentious way gave them proof of his reality. A man who possesses a normal ability to eat food, whose hands and feet they could touch and handle, no matter how difficult it might be to explain how he got into the room, was no ghost. Unquestionably, it was the Jesus they had known before; and the account goes on to say, "Then were the disciples glad when they saw the Lord." (John 20:21)

Eight days after this meeting on Easter evening, Jesus again appeared to the entire apostolic group. Thomas, whose name has since become a synonym for doubter, was present at the time. As he had done previously, Jesus again furnished physical proof of his identity by offering Thomas the opportunity of touching the wounds in his hands and side. The offer itself carried a forceful suggestion of Jesus' telepathic awareness of Thomas' previous declaration of skepticism when he had vehemently declared to the other apostles: "Except I shall see in his hands the print of the nails, and put my finger in the print of the nails, and thrust my hands into his side, I will not believe." It is not clear whether Thomas accepted the offer to touch and handle

Jesus; but the record unmistakably proves that Jesus' actuality was so irresistible as to elicit from the awe-stricken disciple the explosive affirmation, "My Lord! My God!"

The certainty of the men about Jesus that they were dealing with an authentic personality, previously known to them prior to his execution and later objectively manifested among them, is in marked contrast to those who would "existentialize" the resurrection and reduce it to a purely subjective event. Some of the so-called experts deny the objective quality of the appearances and attempt to explain the origin of the Easter Faith as merely the result of "a devout imagination" on the part of the followers of Jesus. As one of them puts it, "The disciples' memory of Jesus quickened to a presence." But there is a shallowness of psychology in all this that is completely unconvincing. These gentlemen of the study are quite defective in historic imagination and are often afflicted by "chronological snobbery"—the notion that it was easier for the contemporaries of Jesus to accept the miracle of a resurrection than it would be for us. But if we may believe the records, the heads of the men about Jesus were as hard as any today.

Following the assassination of Martin Luther King, Jr., it would have been highly improbable if the memory of King had "quickened" to a presence in the minds of his friends and they had gone out seriously asserting that he had returned from the grave and had been seen and talked with on the streets of an American city. This would have been something quite out of the ordinary, to say the least. But it would have been less likely, if within a period of two months, King's friends had succeeded in convincing several thousand of the citizens of Memphis, including members of the police department, the local white clergy, the Ku Klux Klan and other radical right-wing groups, that what they claimed was true. It would be even less conceivable if the friends of King—in spite of threats and intimidations from the city hall, the Governor of the state, the Department of Justice, and the

FBI—had all gone out following King's death in a great missionary movement based on the affirmation of his survival which rapidly spread throughout the country and ultimately became a world religion on which the sun never sets.

The memory of King was impressively strong following his murder—strong enough, in fact, to attract the attention of the entire world and bring many important people from the national establishment and foreign countries to his funeral—but it was hardly powerful enough to produce all these lasting and far-reaching repercussions. This is to put too great a strain on human credulity. By the same token, without the testimony of their physical senses and the "infallible proofs" following the resurrection that Luke speaks of, the disciples would never have been able to believe that Jesus was alive and convincingly preached the fact to others, any more than the friends of Martin Luther King could have done.

An objection frequently advanced against accepting the resurrection as an objective happening is that it is the only one known in human history. However, the same thing may be said about the Sermon on the Mount or the moral character of Jesus. Each is unique in the world's story. If there were several cases, universally admitted, of men who had risen from the dead, no historian would hesitate for a moment on the basis of available evidence to believe that Jesus rose from the dead. It is evident, therefore, that the chief obstacle to accepting the event as an authentic happening lies not in its historicity but in its plausibility. Rudolph Bultmann, whose passion for de-mythologizing the resurrection stories has amounted almost to an obsession, voiced the crux of the matter when he declared: "An historical fact which involves a resurrection from the dead is utterly inconceivable. . . . A corpse cannot come back to life again and climb out of the grave."

According to Bultmann, the resurrection of Christ simply could not have occurred; and therefore, some other explanation must be found to account for the origin of

Christianity. This approach to the problem is not a recent innovation among the biblical elite. The "psychological" theory of the resurrection had its advocates among nineteenth-century critics who began their study of the gospels with the conscious or unconscious acceptance of a negative dogma, the dogma that miracles do not happen, and proceeded to adjust the facts to fit their dogma. One of the first and most widely remembered of these early rationalists who initiated this method of using the tools of form criticism to rob the gospels of their miraculous element was the German critic, David Friedrich Strauss, whose *Leben Jesu* first appeared in 1835 and was translated into English in 1846. Strauss laid down as his canon of New Testament criticism the principle that "in the person and acts of Jesus there was nothing supernatural." He accordingly dates the gospels on the assumption that the miracles must be a later interpolation.

This method has continued in vogue from his time down to the present among many biblical critics who do not test their conclusions by the evidence but test the evidence by its conformity to their beliefs. None of them will go so far as to maintain that the gospels are the work of eyewitnesses who deliberately set down what they knew to be untrue. Instead, those who reject the miraculous element in the New Testament usually maintain one of two positions: (a) the gospels were written by eyewitnesses who mistook for miracles phenomena which are capable of natural explanation; or (b) the gospels were written many years after the events they described by men who were not eyewitnesses of those events. Strauss took the second of these positions; and Paulus, whose *Life of Christ* was published in 1828, took the first.

Paulus adopted the hypothesis that there was nothing miraculous about such acts of Jesus as the Feeding of the Five Thousand. A crowd of greedy people had simply concealed their stores of food but were shamed into sharing them with their hungry neighbors when Jesus and the

Steve: I am sending as many as I can to keep it to 1 oz. I will keep sending them. I have written down all the scripts. and am going to make my own cards out of them. Please send new mem. script. when you find some. IN YOUR OWN TIME. I have plenty to keep me busy for a while.

Numbers 6:24-26   Jamie

apostles began to distribute their own meager supplies. In the
case of Jesus' walking on the water, he contends that it was
merely an optical illusion. Jesus only *seemed* to walk on the
water but in fact was walking on the bank. Strauss was too
realistic to be impressed by such puerilities. "If the gospels,"
he writes, "are genuine historical sources, it is impossible to
eliminate the miraculous from the life of Jesus." And
consequently, he took the position that the gospels were
legendary accounts put together many years after the events
they presumed to describe.

In interpreting the significance of the miraculous element
in the life of Jesus, the words of the Dean of St. Paul's in
London offer a fruitful approach: "I do not believe any
reasonable person would be inclined to assign limits to what
phenomena might accompany the appearance of a
personality which, in any view, was among the most potent
influences which history records." Exceptional things often
happen around exceptional people; and, from a mere human
standpoint alone, we might reasonably expect something of
the nature of miracles to happen around such a personality as
that of Jesus. His resurrection was only the climax of a series
of extraordinary happenings which took place during his
public ministry. The greater part of these were spectacular acts
of healing upon the bodies and minds of men; but certain
others were of an even more impressive character, affecting
inanimate nature. Probably two of the most difficult for the
modern person to fully accept would be those of Jesus'
walking on the water and his stilling the storm on the Sea of
Galilee.

In performing these impressive acts, it is not necessary to
assume that Jesus was contradicting by fiat the basic design
of the natural order. Saint Augustine long ago suggested that
we are not to think of miracles as contrary to nature but only
as contrary to what we *know* of nature. What Jesus did,
therefore, need not be thought of as the rupture of natural
law but instead as the expression of higher laws that we yet
do not comprehend. Even an ordinary human will can

modify the normal course of nature without breaking any natural law. An apple falls from the branch of a tree towards the ground immediately below. Natural law suggests that the apple will inevitably reach the ground unless an agent arrests its passage through the air. Someone puts out his hand and catches the apple. No law of nature is violated. Gravity continues to operate. All that happens is that a human will modified the effects that normally follow when an apple falls to the ground.

The difference between what constitutes the normal and the paranormal is rapidly becoming more difficult to discern. Many things are happening today which a generation ago would have been regarded with as much absolute skepticism as that accorded a resurrection. The truth of William James' statement that "There is no pain in the world like the pain of a new idea" has been amply illustrated by the initial disbelief and skepticism which have often greeted many of the important scientific and technological achievements of the past. When Edison's phonograph was first brought into the meeting of the French Academy of Science in Paris, several members rose and left the room in disgust after hearing it demonstrated; one of them was heard to exclaim on leaving, "How can we sit here and be made fools of by this trickery?" One wonders how this distinguished body of scientists would have reacted at that time, or even in more recent years, to such fantastic accomplishments of the present day as transplanting a human heart, building a computer, or taking a picture of our own earth from a distance of 200,000 miles away.

The modern Sadducee says that it is impossible to believe that Jesus actually walked on water. Twenty-five years ago he doubtless would have said the same about the possibility of a man walking in space. Yet millions of people watching their television sets in the year 1964 witnessed Edward White become the first U.S. astronaut to leave his space capsule and walk out into the empty void. If White walked on space is it inconceivable that Jesus walked on water, even water that was not frozen? If ordinary human beings with their limited abilities—to say nothing of their selfishness and neuroticisms—can build rockets to the moon and control their movements thousands of miles in outer space by the mere turn of a dial, is there any reason to question the fact that a mightier personality, such as that of Jesus, may well have used the eternal laws with more commanding power and controlled by a word a thunderstorm on Galilee? Have there not been rumors coming from the higher levels of expertise that within a few years men may control the weather through technological manipulation?

Amazing things take place around certain individuals with intelligence and the requisite know-how who do not even remotely approach Jesus in the stature and quality of their being. If a lesser human will can modify or control the course of nature in various ways is there any reason why a higher will might not do the same in still more extraordinary ways? That there is no *a priori* objection to miracles is conceded by the eminent agnostic, John Stuart Mill, who says, "The interference of human will with the course of nature is not an exception to law; and by the same rule interference by the divine will would not be an exception, either."

It is not hard to see why the same persons who deny the miracles of Jesus also reject his divinity. Once we accept the reality of his deity, there is no difficulty in believing in his miracles, including that of his resurrection. The resurrection is unique, but Jesus himself is unique. From a naturalistic standpoint, such a life as his could never have happened. He himself is the Sinless Exception; and all lesser miracles become reasonable in the light of his person. His resurrection presents no more unexplainable mystery than does his perfect life. If he rose so majestically above life, it would seem almost inevitable that he should also rise above death. As Henry Drummond once suggested, it may be as natural for a perfect man to rise from the dead as it is for a sinful man to remain in the grave. The crucial issue before present-day Christianity, therefore, seems to be a choice between the historic Christian faith in the Lordship of Jesus Christ, or what Arnold Lunn calls "camouflaged Unitarianism."

In discussing the Incarnation in his book *The Third Day*, Lunn quotes a Roman Catholic writer as saying: "No Catholic teacher would deny that by far the most difficult part of his case for Catholicism is the demonstration of the divinity of Christ, and that once demonstrated, the rest of the apologetic is hardly more than formal. . . . The Catholic schoolmaster holds that the essential part of his apologetics is to persuade his pupils of the truth of the Incarnation, and that accomplished, the rest can almost be left to look after itself." Lunn then goes on to say:

Liberal Protestants, Catholic Modernists, and Anglican Modernists with negligible exceptions believe in the possibility of dissociating Christianity from the belief in miracles. The belief in the *Godhead* of our Lord and the belief in the Resurrection stand and fall together. Those who repudiate the Resurrection have set their feet on a road which leads from Christianity to Unitarianism, open or camouflaged. It is therefore not surprising that modernists who revere Jesus as a mystic, and nothing more, should feel that miracles are a superfluous and distasteful element in the Gospel story. And it may be that this violent prejudice against miracles is, in some cases, inspired by the unconscious realization that the acceptance of miracles implies the acceptance of the Godhead of our Lord.

This is a correct interpretation. The root difficulty of modern theology is a Unitarianism that finds the Christology of the New Testament particularly offensive. The humanist school of today pays lip service to the deity of Christ and his resurrection, primarily at Christmas and Easter, but do not regard either as intrinsically true. Since many Jews accept Christ as "the finest flower of Judaism" but refuse to accept him as the Christ; it is evident that moderns who deny the distinctiveness of Jesus are in reality taking the Jewish and not the Christian position. In fact, a writer in one of our religious publications some time ago quoted an eminent Jewish professor and rabbi as saying that many Christian ministers "are teaching Judaism and don't know it."

The Roman historian Pliny, writing in the first century to the Emperor Augustus, relates how it was the custom of the early Christians to meet together before sunrise on the first day of each week "to sing antiphonally a hymn of praise to Christ as God." There is no excuse for the scissors-and-paste interpretation of the gospels which accepts as authentic those teachings of our Lord which commend themselves to present-day humanists but rejects his reiterated claims to deity. If Jesus Christ were a man, and only a man, then the Christian Church had better go out of business and stop the hypocritical cant of Christian worship.

The heart of the Christian message is the Incarnation of God in Christ, the central fact of the human story; and if this is not true, the church has no gospel to proclaim. If the event did not take place, then let us hush the nonsense of the great glorias and doxologies to "Father, Son, and Holy Ghost." Let us quit observing Christmas and Easter and other great days of the Christian calendar built around the idea. Let us stop mouthing hymns that exalt the deity of Christ with such absurdities as "O come let us adore him, Christ the Lord," "Hail th'incarnate Deity," "O Love Divine, what hast thou done! Th' incarnate God has died for me!" Let the Church quit praying and baptizing in his name, cut out its classical liturgies and sacraments, and stop the foolishness of observing Holy Communion—"this is my body which is broken for you."

If we actually mean one-tenth of what we say in the historic creeds and liturgies of the church, the great hymns of Christendom, the prayers of confession, and all other corporate acts of divine worship which bear witness to him, there does not seem to be any lesser alternative than this. The issue is simply: Do we believe the Christian gospel, or do we prefer the washed-out and attenuated opinions of present-day humanists? If our spiritual assets are limited to a "denatured" Christ, then we are of all men most miserable, for we have no gospel left that has power to redeem.

Unlike the Oriental religions such as Hinduism, Christianity is not primarily a system of philosophy or ethics but an event which occurred at a particular time and place in human history. Professor Walter Raleigh, the agnostic son of a college professor, once arrogantly wrote: "I do not see why philosophy should be made subordinate to certain historical events in Palestine." It is no wonder that the irate professor wrote as he did, for it is precisely at this point where the Christian religion is unique among all the religions of the world.

If Jesus were only a ghostly ideal, born like Hamlet in the brain of Shakespeare, he would still be the greatest ideal on earth, the most valuable dream ever conceived in the mind of man. But how feeble it would be compared to the Christ of history who moves through the pages of the New Testament, who lived an actual human life, died an actual human death, and returned from the grave still retaining all the powers and attributes pertaining to our common humanity. The glory of the Christian religion is that the thing happened. The impossible actually occurred.

The importance of the Great Forty Days in the development and dissemination of Christianity in the world can hardly be overestimated. Luke summarizes the purpose of the period in his introduction to the Book of Acts, stating that Jesus did three things following his resurrection that were of crucial significance:

(a) He showed himself alive after his passion "by many infalliable proofs."

(b) He gave instructions to the apostles whom he had chosen.

(c) He spoke to them about "the things pertaining to the kingdom of God."

One cannot avoid being struck by the fragmentary character of the records dealing with those stirring days. Of all the things that must have been said, only a few sentences have come down to us. With tantalizing brevity, only the main outline of events is suggested. The Lord's final instruction to his disciples that they go and teach "all things whatsoever I have commanded you" certainly implies a corpus of spoken truth far wider in scope than that set down in the four gospels. This body of oral doctrine from the lips of Jesus became a part of the priceless *kerygma*, the cherished memory, of the first-century church and was decisive in the creation of its structure and the course of its future development.

Many things of crucial importance for the continuation of the Christian movement must have taken place during this period; such as that of rebuilding the morale of the disciples following the devastating shock of Jesus' execution, giving specific directions for carrying on the Christian enterprise in the days ahead, and interpreting for the entire group of believers the overall meaning of the crucifixion as Jesus had done for the Emmaus disciples when he gave the two the first rationale of his death ever given to the world and initiated them into the mystery and faith of the cross.

In preparing the disciples for the work ahead, it was necessary that they be convinced of two things. First, they must be certain that Jesus was actually alive and had survived the grave. The proof of this lay in the objectivity of the appearances themselves. The disciples "saw" the Lord and were convinced by the testimony of their physical senses that he was still alive. In no other way would it have been humanly possible for them to have believed. Second, it was necessary that the focus of the disciples' vision be changed from sight to insight; that they must be weaned away from a dependence upon Jesus' physical presence to a confidence in his eternal availability. To do this, it was necessary to develop their powers of spiritual apprehension and intuition so they would no longer need the evidence of their physical senses to believe that he was authentically in their midst.

His repeated appearances to the disciples, followed by

intervals of withdrawal from them, kept the group constantly alert and on the lookout for him. They never knew when to expect him. They might be walking along a lonely road, or by a lakeside fishing, or partaking of a communion meal, and he would appear. Any moment he might be at the door. At no time could they say he was not present, when they were never really sure he had left. This atmosphere of spiritual awareness and expectancy that hung over the apostolic group is vividly portrayed in a passage from Lloyd Douglas' *The Robe*, in which Justus is describing to Marcellus one of the post-crucifixion meetings with Jesus:

"After a while," continued Justus, thickly, "we heard the murmur of voices. We raised our eyes. He was gone."

"Where, Justus? Where do you think he went?" asked Marcellus, huskily.

"I don't know, my friend. I only know he is alive—and I am always expecting to see him. Sometimes I feel aware of him, as if he were close by." Justus smiled faintly, his eyes wet with tears. "It keeps you honest," he went on. "You have no temptation to cheat anyone, or to lie to anyone, or hurt anyone—when, for all you know, Jesus is standing beside you."

"I'm afraid I should feel very uncomfortable," remarked Marcellus, "being perpetually watched by some invisible presence."

"Not if that person helped you to defend yourself against yourself, Marcellus, It is a great satisfaction to have someone standing by—to keep you at your best."

The very thought of a Divine Presence in the souls of men enlightening, strengthening, and elevating them was something new in the experience of mankind. This was the meaning of the Christian doctrine of the Holy Spirit. Never before has such an empowerment for human living been available. The living presence of Jesus has become the inescapable reality of the world and the creative source of moral renewal for the race. A distinguished Jewish rabbi is quoted as having said: "The consciousness of the presence of God has come to millions of men and women through Jesus. He is still the living comrade of countless lives. No Moslem ever sings, 'Mohammed, lover of my soul,' nor does any Jew say to Moses, 'I need thee every hour.' Jesus has brought God near through his presence and has made the Divine personal for myriads of worshippers."

Probably the most significant and impressive of all the visible appearances of Jesus following his resurrection was the one Matthew mentions as taking place on a lonely mountain in Galilee. As we have already noted, Jesus spoke of this meeting before his crucifixion and seemed to attach prime importance to it. As he was leaving the upper chamber where he had eaten the Last Supper with his companions, after warning them of his approaching death, he adds the unique and amazing promise, "Howbeit, after I am risen, I will go before you into Galilee." The understanding at the time seemed to have been that Jesus would meet them there on a specified mountain, doubtless one they were familiar with and could easily identify.

Some biblical authorities who have made careful studies of the geography and history of Palestine during the first century regard Mount Tabor, five miles east of Nazareth, where Jesus was brought up, as the place where the meeting was held. There is substantial evidence to support this view. Its geographic location, as well as certain social and political factors operating at the time, makes Tabor a uniquely appropriate site. In fact, there are not a half dozen other mountains in the whole of Galilee, aside from it, that could possibly fulfill the description.

Dr. James Moffatt, Edgar Goodspeed, and other important Bible scholars hold that this meeting was the same as the appearance to the five hundred that Paul mentions; and the evidence is strongly conclusive that such was the case. In such a tense political climate as that which prevailed after the execution of Jesus, five hundred friends of the hated Galilean could hardly have assembled in the vicinity of Jerusalem without being observed by the Roman or Jewish authorities and the group quickly suppressed as a threat to the peace. Therefore, it was doubtless for this reason that a lonely spot in Galilee, some ninety miles from the capital city, was chosen. Here, the group could come together without attracting the attention of either the authorities at Jerusalem or those of Herod and his court in Tiberias on the Sea of Galilee.

We are only given the barest details of what took place at this meeting, but they are sufficient to suggest that this was one of the most significant gatherings of people ever to take place on earth. It seems to have been in the nature of a commissioning service for the total body of Christ's committed followers who were to represent him in the world. Here the embryo church was commissioned to its world task and given its marching orders from its risen Head. We may be reasonably sure that among the five hundred present on this occasion, in addition to the eleven apostles, there were such devoted friends as Joseph of Arimathea, Nicodemus, Mary Magdalene, Lazarus and his two sisters Martha and Mary, blind Bartimeus whom Jesus had healed, Zaccheus from Jericho, and other stalwart disciples from the towns and villages of Judea and Galilee.

These men and women in their spiritual and representative capacities constituted the leadership of the future Christian church. Upon them rested the responsibility of the Christian enterprise. As emissaries of the risen Lord, they were to bear witness to him and his resurrection throughout the world, many of them sealing their witness to him in their own blood. The effects of this brief scene in the years that have followed has been incalculable. Probably more than any other event recorded in the New Testament, it has kept before the eyes of Christian faith throughout the centuries the vision of a world-wide church and the imperative of the missionary obligation.

Because of its possible connection with this closing scene of Jesus' earthly life, a small party of us on a visit to the Holy Land once took an automobile excursion to the top of Tabor. It was right after we had eaten lunch as guests of the Edinburgh Medical Missionary Hospital in Nazareth that the Arab driver came to the hospital in his well-worn taxi to pick us up for the trip. Two of our friends from the hospital accompanied us on our journey, which led down the slopes of the mountain on which Nazareth is built and five miles southward by the village of Nain, a desolate looking cluster of huts at the foot of a hill where Jesus raised the son of the poor widow. After an hour's visit at Nain, we headed towards Mount Tabor and began a breaktaking ride up the steep and winding road to its summit.

The Arab chauffeur, being a true son of Jehu, drove furiously. Utterly oblivious of the hairpin curves or the absence of guardrails to prevent us from abruptly descending hundreds of feet over impending cliffs, he sped toward the top. I delicately suggested to him that our business was not urgent and that we were not in as great a hurry as he might think. He didn't take the hint. I tried other means of slowing him down. They did not succeed either. Finally when my oblique suggestions failed, I tried the more direct kind and cautioned him to take it easier. But even that failed to work. Nothing seemed to change his resolution or check his movements. Grimly and with demonic glee, he pressed upon the accelerator of the ramshackle vehicle and kept going.

A violent thunderstorm struck us just as we began the climb. The rain beat down upon us and almost blinded our vision. The lightning crashed and the thunder boomed about us; but the old taxi kept groaning and grinding upward with incredible speed. We held grimly on, expecting the worst. However, even the longest road finally comes to an end; and eventually we reached the summit, just as our nerves were at the point of giving out. Then in striking contrast to the ordeal of the ascent, there occurred one of those blessed things known as "serendipity", an unlooked-for something that could only happen half dozen times in a lifetime. The rain ceased just as we arrived at the crest of the mountain, the sun came out; and before our eyes a great rainbow appeared in the sky—one of the richest and most extensive we had ever seen—reaching in a massive arch across the heavens.

It is hardly possible to look at this most mysterious and beautiful phenomenon in all nature without feeling a lift of the spirit. The human heart instinctively leaps up when it sees a rainbow in the sky. But how much more glorious was it to us at the time, standing as we were on the probable spot where the Great Commission was given and the Great Promise was made—the Commission that has inspired the greatest missionary movement in history, and the Promise that has given more hope to Christian believers than any other that ever came from the lips of the Master.

Our hearts were full to overflowing. A deep and urgent sense of purpose came upon us. No outward form was seen, nor audible sound heard; but we were conscious of an Imperial Voice speaking to us across the centuries: "All authority is given me in heaven and in earth. Go ye therefore and teach all nations; and lo, I am with you always, even to the end of the world." As Christ's followers in the twentieth century, we were a part of that living stream of faith that had flowed down the years. We too were commissioned to bear witness to him and to pass on to the world the wonders of his compassion and grace. Likewise, the promise of his unlimited presence was ours also. Unquestionably, as David Livingston once put it, "These are the words of a Gentleman who never broke his promise." To the end of the ages it would ever be thus. He has said so. The sun was going down in a wave of splendor as we ascended the hills that took us back to Nazareth.

CHAPTER SIX

THE MEANING OF THE ASCENSION

On the Mount of Olives, overlooking the old city of Jerusalem three-quarters of a mile away, is the site of the ancient village of Bethany. Here, according to tradition, Jesus took leave of his disciples in a final visit which followed the meeting in Galilee and seemingly was limited to a smaller and more intimate group of the apostles. A church has been built on the site called the Church of the Ascension. From its tower one can see a magnificent panorama of rolling hills stretching for miles in all directions. It is one of the inspiring views of the world and is an appropriate setting for the closing act of Jesus' earthly ministry. As one stands on the spot and views the beckoning horizon, the final words of Jesus spoken to his disciples on the occasion come instinctively to mind: "Ye shall be witnesses unto me both in Jerusalem, and in all Judea, and in Samaria, and unto the uttermost part of the earth." Luke ends his gospel with a description of the event:

"Then Jesus led them out as far as Bethany, and lifting up his hands he blessed them. While he blessed them, he parted from them. And they returned to Jerusalem with great joy, and were continually in the temple blessing God." (24:50-53)

In the Acts of the Apostles we are given additional details of this event not recorded in the Gospel of Luke:

"After saying this, he was taken up into heaven as they watched him, and a cloud hid him from their sight. They still had their eyes fixed on the sky as he went away, when two men dressed in white suddenly stood beside them. 'Men of Galilee,' they said, 'why do you stand there looking up at the sky? This Jesus, who was taken up from you into heaven, will come back in the same way that you saw him go to heaven.' " (1:9-11)

The image of Jesus exalted to the supreme position of power and glory following his crucifixion was the focal point of apostolic preaching. There are frequent allusions to it throughout the New Testament, such as Paul's exhortation to the Christians of Colossae that they "seek those things which are above, where Christ sitteth on the right hand of God"; or, Peter's sermon on the day of Pentecost, when he declared that Jesus who had been crucified and slain by the Jewish leaders had been raised up and "by the right hand of God exalted." A century or more after the crucifixion of Christ, the primitive church formulated a summary statement of its belief which today we call the Apostles' Creed. In that venerable symbol of the faith are the oft-repeated words, "He ascended into heaven and sitteth at the right hand of God the Father Almighty, from thence he shall come to judge the living and the dead." What are we to make of these descriptions?

It should go without saying that the Christian apologists who described Jesus as having ascended to the right hand of God were not speaking literally but metaphorically. They were not undertaking to construct a visual image of their unseen Lord; nor were they attempting to pinpoint a particular location in the universe where he may have gone, as wooden-headed literalists of the "honest to God" sort so solemnly assume. The objective and spectacular aspects of the ascension event as related in the records are noticeably subordinate to its symbolic and religious significance.

There are two cardinal truths in the New Testament associated with the ascension event which are structural in Christian thought. The first of these is that the crucified and risen Jesus is the Lord of history and the controlling power of the future. The second is that he is the full disclosure of God's nature; and between him and God, as the object of man's worship, there is now no longer any practical distinction. The first of these truths was given literary expression in the Book of Revelation; the second became embodied in the Church's doctrine of the Holy Trinity.

In an age of kings, the right hand of the throne was universally recognized as being the focal point of supreme power. When the first Christians spoke of Christ as sitting on the right hand of God, they were proclaiming in figurative terms the conviction that the resurrected Jesus had become a part of the eternal order of the universe and had ascended to the summit and control of all the forces that shape the world; that "the glory and majesty and dominion and authority" which are God's alone belong to Christ also.

In the year 96 A.D., during the reign of the Roman Emperor Domitian, a great persecution of Christians took place; and it looked for a time as though Christianity itself might be completely blotted out. Some years before this, a cult of emperor-worship, similar to that of Japanese Shintoism prior to World War II, had arisen. Temples were built in honor of the reigning emperor; and Christians, as an act of loyalty to the state, were required to offer incense before his image. This, many of them refused to do; and throughout the provinces, Domitian had ordered his emissaries to compel the Christians to submit or be executed.

It was during this time of bitter suffering that the little Christian community produced one of the most remarkable literary productions ever written, the Book of Revelation. Its author was a Christian named John—though certainly not the Apostle John as it is sometimes claimed—who had been exiled to a penal colony off the coast of Asia Minor. It was probably while working in the rock quarries of this ancient concentration camp that the inspired vision came to him. The book was written and circulated among the churches for the purpose of giving hope and encouragement to the greatly distressed Christians of that day, and to nerve the early church for its inevitable clash with the world-wide might of Rome.

The author depicts himself as standing on the lonely Island of Patmos, amid the confusion and mysteries of time, and seeing through an open door, a throne set in heaven. In the right hand of One who sat upon the throne was a book—the Book of Destiny, containing the hieroglyphics of the future and sealed with seven mystic seals. A voice calls out of heaven saying, "Who is worthy to open the book and to loose the seals thereof?" Heaven and earth are searched to find someone worthy to break the seals that hold in secret the divine councils, but no one is found. Then the inspired writer breaks into weeping because no man is forthcoming who is worthy to open the book, nor even so much as to look thereon.

At this juncture, one of the heavenly attendants comes to him and says, "Weep not. Behold the Lion of the Tribe of Judah of the root of David has prevailed to open the book and to loose the seven seals thereof." The apostle turns to see this Lion whose mystic strength could reveal and shape the future. Instead, as the symbol of ultimate power, he sees the meekest and most helpless of all creatures, a Lamb with the marks of slaughter upon it. Then follows one of the most daring and sublime affirmations of the place of Christ in the moral universe in all sacred literature. The Lamb approaches the throne and, with sublime audacity, takes the Book of Destiny out of the hand of him who sat thereon and breaks its seals. Then the hierarchy of heaven falls before him in worship and the angelic choirs break forth into an ascription of divine honor to the Slain Lamb.

The earliest form of confession used by the primitive church was the simple formula, "Jesus is Lord!" This is the central idea of the Book of Revelation. Its basic conviction is that Jesus represents the way the universe is put together; that the universe is God's, and that anyone or anything that is set up against his Christ will be destroyed. The heavenly scene is a symbolic description of the fundamental nature of reality. The imagery of the Slain Lamb is a dramatic portrayal of the fact that the principle of sacrificial love is as deeply embedded in the spiritual world as gravity is in the physical world; and that in Jesus Christ and his cross is embodied the ultimate power of the universe.

This is not the concept of power that is now generally held. At a certain popular resort in San Francisco is a huge oil painting commemorating Pearl Harbor. It is a pictorial sermon on the text, "Trust God and keep your powder dry." Its background shows a magnificent sun just coming up and splendorizing all the clouds with glory, while in the foreground is a massive air-and-sea armada pouring out of the Golden Gate in an avalanche of battleships, torpedo boats, and bombing planes to avenge Pearl Harbor. The title of the picture—a gross prostitution of the closing words of the Lord's Prayer—"The Power and the Glory." The painting is an apt illustration of the false concept of power abroad in the world and a parable of the blasphemous pride of man revealed in its crude and overweening arrogance.

The question of the meaning of power is one of the most pressing issues of the present day. The outcome of man's search for physical security rests ultimately upon the question of what constitutes power. It is generally regarded that things spiritual are weak and ineffective. Truth, justice, and mercy are qualities to be admired and praised but are too fragile in themselves to count for much in the practical decisions of men and nations. Some years ago, in answer to a question in the British Parliament as to what the government ought to base its foreign policy on, a leading spokesman of the Labour Party replied that it ought to base its policies on the Sermon on the Mount. At this, an old admiral blurted out, "If that is what we are going to do, all I've got to say is 'God help us!' " to which the speaker replied, "He will."

It is this false notion of what constitutes power that dominates the unimaginative troglodyte minds of the military who now shape our national policy. The preamble of the

UNESCO charter says, "Wars begin in the minds of men; and it is in the minds of men that the defenses of peace must be constructed." If mankind is to survive, it must change substantially its manner of thinking. It must rid itself of the deadly delusion that massive weaponry represents a real defense against foreign aggression; that violence can be successfully used to overcome violence; and that brute force is the final arbiter and disposer of our destiny.

In the picture John gives us in Revelation we see the overweening power of a great world-state, incarnate in such emperors as Nero and Domitian, demanding the worship of their subjects. Ancient emperor-worship has its counterpart in the present-day cult of nationalism which Fosdick called "man's other religion." Ancient idolatry made for itself a graven image, and bowed down to it; the modern pagan makes an image of the state, and worships it in the name of patriotism. Against both are the awful words of the living God, "Thou shalt have no other God before me!"

Dr. Arnold Toynbee brings out the fact that modern nationalism offers a sinister threat to man's well-being today, and says: "Our states have become our principal Gods in practice, though states are not really Gods, but are simply public utilities like roads, drains, and installations for supplying gas, electricity and water. This present form of idolatry is a threat to the survival of the human race in the atomic age. Mankind's most pressing problem today is to find ways and means to reduce to the safety level the charge of emotion attaching to the symbols we call states."

Preparation for war is a major concern of the most powerful nations today. The Great Beast of Nationalism demands our utmost allegiance and the deployment of the bulk of our national resources on so-called security measures, while works of mercy and compassion go begging. The mammoth consortia of power represented by the military system constitute man's supreme corporate defiance of God and the greatest challenge to the rule of Christ on earth. No moral issue today compares with the morality of warfare and the preparation for it, for in these preparations man usurps the prerogative of God and attempts to play the part of God himself. Dr. Charles Clayton Morrison, in an editorial in *The Christian Century* some years ago, defined war as a human project intended to force God's hand—an insolent attempt on the part of man to dissolve his partnership with God and wrest the control of history from the hands of the Lord of history.

The great problem of trusting God at the present time is connected with the fact of war. The problem is essentially no different from that of trusting God in the home or neighborhood, but the issue is on a vaster scale. War is a denial of a trust in God. It is a defiance of the processes of history, for to trust God means to trust the pacific processes of God in history—the processes that make for peace, for fellowship, for justice, for goodwill. This, men refuse to do when they take matters into their own hands and attempt by force of arms to coerce the course of human events into the channel of their national self-interests and aggrandizement.

Man's part in the world process, according to Dr. Morrison, is to find out what God is doing in the historic continuum of living experience and to cooperate with it. The clew to God's action is in the revelation of God's character which appeared to us in Jesus Christ. What Jesus did in the limited sphere of his earthly history, God does in the vast ranges of history and throughout all ages; therefore, trusting God is "to believe that God is doing in the full circle of history what Jesus did in his tiny arc of history—to believe this and cooperatively to act upon it."

Mounting stockpiles of hydrogen bombs, the fleet of Polaris submarines, and our anti-ballistic missile systems on which we are spending astronomical sums suggest that our ultimate trust for security is in military force, rather than in the God and Father of our Lord Jesus Christ. One can almost hear the ancient pagan inquiry concerning the massive buildup: "Who is like unto the Beast; Who is able to make war with him?" However, the anachronism of the modern war system is becoming increasingly evident. Two basic insights as to its fundamental nature are being brought out as never before. The first of these is that war is inherently and totally immoral; and the second is that it is futile, or as the French would say, "It is worse than evil, it's stupid."

Of all the vast horrors that haunt the race, war is the least rational and the most destructive of physical and spiritual values. Despite all rationalizations and pious equivocations used to justify military ventures in the past, the moral judgment of mankind now knows that if there is anything in the world ethically wrong at the present time it is war. If murder is wrong, then war is wrong; for war is simply organized mass murder. Bring all the evils of mankind together—including killing, lying, stealing, adultery, arson, rape and torture—concentrate them into one package and scatter them continent-wide and world-wide and this is war. War is the distilled essence of all evils, on an unprecedented scale, and with the compulsion and sanction of government behind it. Walt Whitman called it "a vast diarrhea." The very heart of the Christian gospel is denied and betrayed by those who would justify or condone such evil. Contrast Christ's commandment to love with this description of the Hiroshima blast:

"Crowds of maddened people," said one atom bomb survivor, "were running like demented lemmings . . ., screaming, and it sounded like one enormous voice. . . . Their skins hung from them like strands of dark seaweed. Instead of noses, holes! Their ears and hands were so swollen as to be shapeless. . . . In the terror of their dying, they clawed their way over one another, their eyes hanging from their sockets, pushing one another in the river and screaming all the time."

Or take this description of the "pacification" program of Vietnamese villagers, written by the news reporter, George Orwell:

The Vietnamese woman ignored the crying baby in her arms. She stared in hatred at the American infantrymen with shotguns blazing away at chickens and ducks. Others shot a water buffalo and a pet dog. While her husband, father, and young son were led away, the torch was put to the hut that contained the family belongings. The flames consumed everything—including the shrine to the family ancestors.

The first casuality in any war is truth; the second is compassion. Modern warfare has descended to such depths of obscenity as to cause thousands of individuals and groups throughout the world to renounce it and take the complete pacifist position. One of the early such persons was the late Dr. Albert Einstein who, on his return to Germany from Switzerland during World War I, termed the war "senseless violence" and declared, "I had rather be smitten to shreds than to participate in such doings." All justifications and rationalizations which have heretofore been used in defense of the war system are now unrealistic, irrelevant, and irresponsible.

A second insight which is forcing itself upon us today is that war is not only ethically wrong but colossally idiotic as well. As a problem-solving device, it unfailingly fails to attain the ends it sets out to accomplish. Henryk Sienkiewicz, the author of the great classic *Quo Vadis*, has said there are two infinite things in the universe: the infinite stupidity of man, and the infinite charity of God. Nowhere is the first of these imponderables more in evidence than in man's employment of the war system as a means for the attainment of moral ends. War represents the n-th degree of human idiocy. Its madness and futility are illustrated by a remark made to Peter Arnett, a journalist in Vietnam, by a prominent American officer who sought to justify a certain military operation with the explanation, "We had to destroy the village in order to save it."

Whether or not Christianity may be regarded as a true and

workable way of life, in the light of such lunacies as the above, done in the name of realism and moral purpose, there should be no longer any question about the falsity of its opposite. Current events reveal the fact that Caesar is not mocking Christ but that Caesar is being shown up as the brutal and stupid nitwit that he is. The boasted realism of many so-called realists in policy-making positions of power is proving to be the most crackpot thing on earth.

Power is not a static but a functional thing. It is the ability to accomplish purpose. A person has power to the degree he is able to do what he wants or intends to do. If he cannot accomplish his purpose, even though he has physical power comparable to that of a thousand hydrogen bombs, he is as though he has no power at all, for the power he has is not relevant to his purpose. The effectiveness of the means may be judged by the ends sought. There are some things that are good for one thing but quite useless for another. A typewriter is good for writing a letter but no good for cultivating a garden; a stick of dynamite can wreck a building but it is powerless to destroy an idea; an H-bomb can devastate a city but it cannot create goodwill.

Military force, heretofore regarded as the ultimate device for implementing foreign policy and restraining aggression, is proving to be no power at all; for it is the wrong kind of power to attain the goals that civilized peoples desire for themselves and others. We affirm that our national purpose is a just and lasting peace, freedom, democracy, liberty and justice for ourselves and others. Fortunately, our land is not alone in its noble declaration, for all the other nations avow the same objectives. Yet we undertake to accomplish these ends by the use of the futile and archaic tools of military coercion and brute force which eventually bring these objectives to naught.

A leading American psychologist has pointed out that national states today are manifesting extreme symptoms of paranoia that are similar to those of mental patients who see their problems but select means of solving their difficulties which only aggravate them. Rival nations vie with each other in creating obscene weapons of war for the purpose of keeping the world peaceful. We pile up huge armaments with the idea of attaining security but we only get insecurity. We set out to stop communism by force of arms and only succeed in making more Communists. An idea like that of communism cannot be stopped by bullets any more than one can shoot a ghost. You can kill individual Communists; but you can't kill an idea except by replacing it with a better idea. Military power is completely irrelevant, either for the purpose of producing peace or stopping aggression. There are fifty different ways intelligent people have of putting out a fire, but pouring gasoline on the blaze is not one of them.

Armaments no longer afford any security; instead, they have become our greatest threat. As Einstein pointed out a short time before his death, "The national state is obsolete, for it can no longer protect its citizens." Nations now have the ability to destroy but not to defend. All talk of saving civilization by war is irrational. How can modern civilization be more utterly destroyed than by war? It is as impossible to cure the ills of the world through organized bloodshed and mass destruction as it is to cure a child's colic by throwing a bomb into the nursery.

The truth of George Bernard Shaw's observation that "though we crucified Christ on a stick, he somehow managed to get hold of the right end of it" is being amply illustrated on the contemporary scene. There is a reality of "power politics"; but there is also the reality of the moral law. In the death and resurrection of Christ the nature of the moral order has become clear. Moral power, directed in the interest of moral purpose, is the ultimate force in the universe because the nature of things backs it up. A favorite statement of the late Martin Luther King, Jr., who drew his principles of non-violence from Christianity and Mahatma Gandhi, was to the effect that Christ showed us the way and Gandhi showed us it would work.

Any system of political power that runs contrary to the

nature of power as revealed in Jesus Christ is bound to fail. There is a punitive principle at work in the world by which men and nations are punished for their sins by the inexorable operation of the forces imminent in history itself. National governments, in their blind arrogance, act as though they are superior to the moral law, and can violate it with impunity. But they are mistaken: both men and nations reap what they sow.

The present troubles of the world are not a denial of the presence of God but the affirmation of it. They are simply the revelation of the law of cause and effect: you can't make a fool out of God. If a man could violate all the laws of health and still be healthy; if he could sow weeds and still get wheat; if he could build his skyscrapers contrary to the law of the perpendicular and they would continue to stand up; or if he could cheat, and lie, and steal and still feel inwardly secure and happy, then one might well ask, Where is God and what is he doing?

But the inescapable fact of human existence is that the more we oppose the will of God the more the will of God opposes us; or, as the psalmist would say, "The face of the Lord is against those who do evil." We speak of breaking the law of God; but this is not a strictly accurate statement. Men cannot break the moral law any more than they can break the law of gravity. They simply illustrate it—all of which goes to show that the universe is foolproof but the fools have not found it out yet.

The world is confronted with the momentous choice of brotherhood or annihilation. Mankind must give up the war system or perish. It would seem that God is trying to create in man a will to peace which will make him want peace more than anything else heretofore considered valuable; to prefer it to profits, or jobs, standards of living, national glory, or any other lesser aims. Oddly enough, the power of enlightened self-interest has now become a powerful spiritual force working on behalf of international cooperation and brotherhood.

All national states are controlled not by idealism or moral purpose as they usually claim, but by their self-interest. No treaty or international agreement is ever kept between two nations unless it is mutually beneficial to each. They may not keep their agreement because it is honorable or right; but they will keep it if it is profitable for them to do so. This principle of self-interest now operates as a contributing motivation for peace, since in the event of war, the victor nation finds it necessary to act as saviour of the vanquished. The interrelatedness of mankind and the necessity for international trade make it imperative that the defeated nation be put back on its feet economically, since it is a physical impossibility to trade with a graveyard.

There is an order of peace that contends with the order of war. At the opening of the Pasteur Institute in Paris, Louis Pasteur spoke of two laws in the world that struggle for supremacy and said:

Two contrary laws stand today opposed: one a law of blood and death, which, inventing daily new means of combat, obliges the nations to be ever prepared for battle; the other a law of peace, of labor, of salvation, which strives to deliver man from the scourges which assail him. One looks only for violent conquest; the other for the relief of suffering humanity. The one would sacrifice hundreds of thousands of lives to the ambition of a single individual; the other places a single human life above all victories. The law of which we are the instruments essays even in the midst of carnage to heal the wounds caused by the law of war.

The two wars which Pasteur referred to continue in progress. There is the way of annihilation or the way of active goodwill. Without an equal growth of mercy and compassion, men's scientific achievements can destroy all that makes life liveable on this planet. For this reason, it is imperative that internationally there be formulated a massive course of action to conform to this concept based on the needs of the world and the well-being of mankind.

The real war of humanity is against hunger, ignorance, disease and war itself. It is not generally realized that over half of mankind does not possess beds and tables, knives or forks; much less radios, refrigerators and automobiles. Three out of five persons living in the world today have an income of $40 a year, and hardly a quarter of these can read or write; few have enough food to keep soul and body together and on an average will not live past thirty.

The late Dr. Frank C. Laubach, the great "Apostle of Literacy" whom Norman Cousins called "one of the noblest human beings of our time" and whose simplified "each one teach one" method of teaching literacy has enabled over 60 million adults speaking 200 different languages to read and write, speaks of the vast and ever-widening imbalance between the rich nations which are getting richer and the poor nations which are getting poorer. In his recent book, *Forty Years with the Silent Billion*, he says:

More than half of the human race is hungry, driven, diseased, afraid of educated men in this world and of demons in the next. I have not only seen these people across Asia and Africa, but have sat beside many of them and taught them one by one, and have seen a new light kindle in their eyes; love and hope began to dawn as they stepped out of their blindness and began to read. I know that we could free the multitudes from their tragic bondage. . . . The illiterates are *frantic to learn.* . . .The communists find them easy, but we can find them just as easy. *Anybody* can have them who lifts them out of ignorance and poverty. . . . The astonishing landing on the moon showed what modern science can do when 300,000 men work together. Removing the awful lop-sidedness of the world would be easier than reaching the moon. We have all the science and technology we need. All we need now is the burning heart that loves others as we love ourselves.

Dr. Laubach was personally instrumental in influencing President Truman to adopt the Point IV Program for sharing our scientific and technological knowledge with the backward nations of the world. In his Inaugural address on January 20, 1949, the President advocated a program for making "the benefits of our scientific advances and industrial progress available for the improvement and growth of undeveloped areas . . . to produce more food, more clothing, more material for housing, and more mechanical power to lighten their burdens." The Point IV Program which was passed by Congress was later adopted by the United Nations and is now the objective of that body.

This was the first comprehensive assault on world hunger and need; but the financial support of it is insignificant compared with the amounts spent each year on armaments. Few people are aware that the total cost of the United Nations for one year, including all of its subsidiary agencies such as the World Health Organization and the Point IV Program, is less than one day's cost of World War II; and that the United States pays less to the operating budget of the United Nations than does New York City for its annual garbage collection.

The price of peace is no longer power but justice. We must lift the world or lose it. Cooperation with God at the present time requires a Christian internationalism that is willing to trust our future destinies in the broader areas of the world, as in our personal lives, to the controlling hand of God as he is revealed in Jesus Christ. There are great divine pressures compelling men to live cooperatively or perish. Someone has suggested that the church, as the corporate instrument of God's purpose in the world, must make up its mind whether Jesus Christ as Head of the Church shall *lead* us as Saviour to the goal of brotherhood and peace or *drive* us as the Lord of history—whether we are impelled to this high goal "by the hands of love or the iron chains of necessity."

It has never been the divine method to nullify the will of man, or take away his freedom of choice, thus making him into a mere pawn. But there is an alternative to this. There remains the compulsion of the real. The nature of things is such that men are tied together in an inescapable humanity so that no one can destroy or neglect his brother without destroying himself. This truth of man's interrelationship and inexorable interdependence, heretofore only dimly recognized, is now being brought out by cumulative circumstances so clearly and convincingly that eventually men may no longer be able to deny the truth any more than they can deny the sun in heaven. In this case, mankind would be confronted by a divine *fait accompli* which would not destroy his essential freedom of choice but, instead, would compel him by the coercion of reality.

God is shutting man up to every false way of escape. In spite of his proud boastfulness, mankind is rapidly being maneuvered into the position that the ancient prophets were always trying to get Israel to accept—that of complete mistrust of self and absolute reliance on God. In his overweening pride man would not listen to God. Now he must listen to him in helplessness and despair. Events are beating him to the earth; but in this fact there is hope. Despair can be creative when it turns men to God.

The pre-eminent and unending reign of Christ as the Lord of history is the first great truth of the ascension. The New Testament speaks of the power and influence of Jesus in terms of eternal rule. He is not only represented as sitting at the right hand of God, but the confident assertion is that he will remain there until all opposition to his spirit and rule is brought under divine control. A contemporary expression of this fact was given at the crowning of Elizabeth II of England. During the coronation services at the high altar of Westminster Abbey, the young queen returned down the blue-carpeted aisle holding her scepter in the right hand and in her left a circular gold object surrounded by a cross of jewels. It was the royal orb, used in every coronation. When it was delivered to her, it was delivered with these words: "Receive the orb set under the cross, and remember that the whole world is subject to the power and empire of Christ our Redeemer."

It was this truth which was the central theme of the Book of Revelation and the hard-core teaching of the early apostles as they spoke of Jesus' exaltation to the right hand of God. The primitive church was simply saying in effect, "Don't overlook the Crucified! The scepter of the universe is in these pierced hands."

When Christ stepped behind the veil of matter at his ascension, he did not leave the world but continued as the controlling influence that shapes the future. Having once grasped the scepter of universal power, he has kept it; and there does not seem to be any serious likelihood of his ever relinquishing it. The great things that are happening in the world today are not happening in Washington or Moscow, London or Peking but in the higher spheres of reality where the great matters are determined, and from which the eternal forces of truth and righteousness and justice flow. While the conflict on earth is important, and our every conscious act has enormous significance, yet it is in the unseen realm where the great strategies are being determined. Divine reign means that the controlling powers of history come from the source where will and power are one.

Through his death, resurrection, and ascension Christ has opened the kingdom of heaven to all believers. In spite of all the challenging obstacles that threaten the world in the future—the madness and insanity of war, the cries of race and clan, the injustices and oppressions of the toiling masses, the callousness and brutality of great power structures—he must reign until he has put all enemies under his feet. He is the King of the kingdom of God and all lesser kingdoms must give way to his. Thus "heaven grows, and yet is never filled, and the wheat is sifted from the chaff."

The second great meaning of the ascension is that Jesus Christ is the personalized expression, not only of ultimate power, but also of ultimate goodness. When the early Christians spoke of Jesus as being at the right hand of God, they were proclaiming the fact that in his death, resurrection, and exaltation he had risen to the apex and control of men's thoughts about God. "The church catholic and universal," says the late Dr. John A. Hutton, former editor of *The British Weekly*, "has clung to the faith that lights up our desperate necessities—that Jesus Christ has for us sinful men changed the Face of God into his own, with God's consent."

This statement represents the truth of the matter. The impression Jesus has made on the thought of the race is so complete that it is impossible for a Christian to pray without thinking of him. In our highest moments of insight and devotion, when thoughts of God are uppermost in the mind, it is the face of the human Christ that becomes the central image and focal point of our thoughts. A billion people, or one-third of the human race, close their prayers in his name.

Someone has suggested that if the noblest spirits of the race should sit down and attempt to think out the kind of God they would like to see in the universe, his moral and spiritual likeness would gradually form like unto the Son of Man. The highest description of human character in any language is the adjective "Christlike." When India, a non-Christian nation, wanted to pay the highest compliment to her greatest son, she called Gandhi a Christlike man. In terms of ethics, Jesus has become the norm of human behavior so completely that men cannot form a conception of the right without taking him into account.

The first Christians were confronted by a Man whose existence in the world made them certain of God. It was this fact out of which the idea of Trinity arose. The doctrine of the Trinity was an attempt on the part of early Christian thinkers to relate the human Jesus to the structure of eternal reality. The question which challenged these men was: How can Christ have for us the value and reality of God, without being God? How may the statement that Jesus is Lord be reconciled with the truth that God is one? The history of Christian thought during the first four centuries is the story of a long and agonizing debate over the correct way of conceptualizing the relationship between Jesus and God and expressing in systematized, metaphysical terms the truth of the Incarnation. In its formulation of the ancient creeds the church was attempting to safeguard its belief in the Lordship of Jesus without disrupting the truth of the essential unity of the Godhead.

The Trinity is a description of God's three-fold manifestation of himself in history. The doctrine of Father, Son, and Holy Spirit does not signify three persons in the sense we use the term today but, rather, three manifestations of one and the same reality. The Latin "persona," from which the word "person" was derived, originally meant the mask worn by an actor on a Roman stage. In the oldest form of Greek drama, from which the Roman originated, there was only one actor and a chorus. Later another actor was added. An actor at one time might impersonate the king, at another the queen and at still another a slave or domestic. The Romans called the mask he wore a *per sona*, or something that one sounded through in depicting each separate impersonation. Thus, at the present time, in singing the hymn "God in three persons blessed Trinity," we need to keep in mind that its meaning is not "person" in the modern sense of the word but in the Latin sense of persona, or "modes of being." In other words, the doctrine of the Trinity was the attempt of the church's greatest thinkers to describe what Karl Barth called "God's three ways of being God."

Two analogies may help to illuminate this concept. The first is from Patristic thought and is Ruffinus' illustration of spring, fountain, and stream. The Spring, God the Father, Source and Creator, sends forth the Fountain (the Son) to incarnate the water's glory; while "proceeding from both" —Spring and Fountain—flows the Stream (the Spirit). All is the same water—one in essence in Spring, Fountain, and Stream—but a Trinity in expression.

The second analogy of the Trinitarian truth is the illustration of the way it is possible for one person to know another—such, for example, as that of the composer, Mozart.

Barth was so inordinately fond of Mozart's music that he once declared that when he got to heaven he would pass up all his friends among the preachers and theologians and after meeting the Saviour he would look up Mozart. Had Barth lived contemporaneously with the great composer he might have known Mozart in one or all of three different ways. He could have known him through a study of his written music, or by hearing him play and enjoying his skill as an interpretive artist, or by knowing him intimately as a personal friend. In these roles Mozart would have been expressing his three-fold "personae" and revealing himself to Barth in three separate characters—as composer, performer, and friend.

These illustrations, like all illustrations, are inadequate to express the whole truth; but they do help us to understand what the church fathers were attempting to say about the nature of God. These early theologians who formulated the doctrine certainly did not presume to say that God was one person composed of three persons. They were not mathematical idiots. To say that three personalities can add up to one personality would, of course, be nonsense. What they did say was simply this: God the Eternal, the one Supreme Being, revealed himself in human experience in three separate ways, or as three personae.

But the question may be asked: Granted that all this is true, why bother about such an abstract and theoretical matter? What practical value for human living does the doctrine of the Trinity hold for men and women of the present? People generally regard theology as something so far removed from everyday experience as to be of slight interest to any but professional theologians. Someone has said that when a person is speaking about something he does not understand, to a group of people who do not understand him, upon a subject that if they did understand it would not make a particle of difference in the world to anybody present, that is theology.

But this is to underrate the importance of logical, systematized concepts as compared with muddled or confused ones. Theology is the serious attempt to formulate in the truest and best terms man's highest thought about God. If we disregard theology, this does not mean that we have no ideas about God. It may mean that we have a lot of wrong ones—mixed-up, out-of-date ideas. The truth is that most of the ideas about God which are put forth as novelties today are simply old worn-out ones which the great theologians have already tried centuries ago and discarded.

Much may be said in criticism of the abstract and speculative treatment given the dogma of the Trinity in the past. There has probably been more sheer nonsense spoken and written about it than any other item in the Christian belief. Thomas Jefferson complained of "the incomprehensible jargon" of Trinitarian theology of his day; and Jefferson himself was a pretty smart fellow. The arguments in support of it have often appeared to be merely theological hair-splitting; and in incompetent hands, the truth has suffered serious distortion and has been subjected to gross misapprehensions. But this is not to say that the belief itself is unimportant.

Theology has a much more practical bearing upon our everyday lives than is commonly supposed. Man's destiny rests ultimately upon what kind of God is running the show. What a man believes about God is the most decisive factor in determining his conduct. The basic difficulty with the Aztec Indians of Mexico in the time of Cortes was their distorted idea of God, which expressed itself in the practice of human sacrifice. It was this fatal depravity, rooted in a false concept of deity, that brought about the downfall of Aztec civilization, an otherwise advanced culture. This historic illustration simply indicates how theoretical matters do take practical turns. We may not always be aware of the connection between daily living and the Second Law of Thermodynamics or the Quantum Theory; but much of present-day technology is based on them, including such down-to-earth objects as dynamos, telephones, and refrigerators.

The most important question in religion is what is God like. It is not only essential that we believe in a God; even more crucial is what *kind* of a God do we believe in? How shall we think of him? The doctrine of the Trinity is man's highest attempt to come to grips with the nature of ultimate reality and to give an answer to the question which contains within itself the answer to all questions. An illustration from a physics class during the writer's college days will furnish background for the awesome matter.

On this particular occasion, the professor of physics was addressing a group of young Aristotles on the laws of motion by describing how all the planets, carrying their respective moon satellites, were in regular motion around the sun; how the earth itself was spinning like a merry-go-round on its axis at the rate of over a thousand miles an hour, and at the same time sailing through space on its annual journey around the sun at a speed of 18½ miles per second. While this was going on, we were told that the sun itself was speeding on its massive flight through space at the tremendous velocity of 43,000 miles an hour, carrying with it the earth and eight other major planets and their satellites, thousands of asteroids, a thousand comets, and millions of meteors—all moving in the direction of the great star Vega.

All of this was quite frightening and disturbing enough in itself; but the class was informed that it did not exhaust the matter, for there was a fourth motion involving the earth which we usually do not consider. The Milky Way, our own galactic system of some 100,000 light years across, is turning at an incredible speed about a central axis located in the direction of the constellation Sagittarius, the system being so immense as to require some 200,000,000 years to rotate once upon its axis. At this point in the lecture, the professor paused and with impressive solemnity said, "Young ladies and young gentlemen, every object in the universe known to man is in motion except the throne of God."

In the moment of silence which followed this momentous announcement, science and religion seemed to blend together in an overwhelming reality of fact. At least one member of the group left the class that morning with an awesome sense of the "ebb and flow of ever enduring power" subsisting at the heart of physical creation; and a feeling that we mortals probably know little more about the Universal Mind, and the total design of the universe, than a fly crawling around on the score of Beethoven's Seventh Symphony knows of the purpose and mind of the great composer.

The Christian religion carries its definitive description of reality in two stupendous affirmations about God, both of which are embodied in its doctrine of the Trinity. The first truth is that God is personal. The broad basis of Christian belief is that the throne of the universe is not vacant, as the materialists hold, but is occupied by a supreme Being who is the creative power and energy of all things—"Himself unmoved, all motion's source." There are persons who believe that nothing exists except nature and that everything that *is* has always existed or else has come into existence as a result of blind forces. They are called naturalists. There are others who affirm that there is something in and above nature that brought it into being. They are known as super-naturalists. Among this latter group are the Christians, who hold that the Power which "creates, sustains, and orders all" is personal.

For this reason, the Bible used the pronouns He, His, Him, Thou and Thine in its description of this supreme Power. When Moses at the Burning Bush questioned the divine Voice which had commanded him to lead the Israelites out of Egypt he said, "When I come unto the children of Israel and shall say unto them, The Lord God of your fathers, the God of Abraham, the God of Isaac, and the God of Jacob hath sent me unto you and they shall say to me, What is his name? What shall I say unto them?" The answer given Moses contained the startling word "I," which is an expression of the very essence of personality: "And God said unto Moses, I AM THAT I AM. Thus shalt thou say unto the children of Israel, I AM hath sent me unto you. This is my name forever and my memorial unto all generations." (Ex. 3:14)

The materialist Haeckle replaced God by a primal substance which he crowned the Emperor of the universe under the title Mobile Cosmic Ether. To him, God was only a cosmic "wiggle," a blind unthinking force which Thomas Hardy described as "the dreaming dark Dumb Thing that turns the handle of this empty show." Thus, for the naturalist, the ultimate power that controls nature is impersonal and is not aware of the life process. It knows nothing and cares nothing about what goes on. The difference between the naturalist and the supernaturalist might be expressed by the crucial question: Is God aware of what he is doing? If God knows what he is doing, then he transcends all his works. If he does not know what he is doing, then he is less than man, and to worship something less than man is idolatry. It is as great a sacrilege to worship a blind force or stream of energy as it is to bow down to an idol of wood or stone. Both are pitiful expressions of human blindness and folly.

An impersonal God would not deserve man's worship, for in so doing man would prostrate himself before something that was inferior to himself. There are some who hesitate to attribute personality to God lest they limit him thereby and reduce him to a mere anthropomorphism. This is a justifiable caution which the Old Testament takes account of when it declares, "My thoughts are not your thoughts, saith the Lord; for as the heavens are high above the earth, so are my thoughts higher than your thoughts and my ways higher than your ways." However, we need to keep in mind the fact that this is a minimal and not a maximal description of God's nature. The Biblical view of God as personal does not presume to limit him, nor to say all there is to be said about him in the higher aspects of his being. What it does say, however, is that whatever else God may be, he is greater than all his works; and is certainly not less, but infinitely more, than anything he has created, including man himself.

The second great affirmation of Christianity is that the infinite and unfathomable Being who occupies the universal throne, who made the stars and the great galaxies and knows them all by name as a shepherd knows his sheep, has been revealed in a human life. The Apostle Paul expresses the great truth in a matchless sentence: "For God, who commanded the light to shine out of darkness, hath shined in our hearts to give the light of the knowledge of the glory of God in the face of Jesus Christ." Christianity is structured on the incomprehensible fact that the creative Source of all energy and power was once focused in human form.

The idea of the Trinity did not emerge as a purely speculative construct but had its roots in the experience of the early Christians. There was a Trinity of experience before there was a Trinity of doctrine. The concept did not spring out of dogma; rather, the dogma sprang out of the experience of God which came to men in their encounter with the historic Jesus. The vision of God which he brought represented a new dimension of reality; and as a result, the first Christians began to think of the supreme object of their worship in terms of a threeness. He was the God who was *above* them as the creative source of all; the God who was *among* them in the Jesus of history; and the God who was *within* them as an inspiring and empowering Spirit. This new idea of God became embodied in the worship of the early church and was incorporated into its doxologies, its prayers, and its varied liturgy; holy baptism was administered in the three-fold Name; and the closing words of their communal fellowship, when Christians said goodbye to one another, were: "The grace of our Lord Jesus Christ, the love of God, and the communion of the Holy Spirit be with you all."

The early Christian thinkers regarded the doctrine of the Trinity as a theological formula which expressed the essential truths of the Christian faith in one comprehensive statement. They held to it not because they could explain it, but because it helped to explain everything else. It became a key to the nature of reality, a conceptualization of the living truth which underlies both the natural and the spiritual world. In formulating it, they were trying desperately to uphold two seemingly opposite descriptions about the nature of the Divine: They were attempting to say that God was authentically present in Christ (or as much of him as could be focussed in a human life); and, at the same time, that God was one. Logically, they could not reconcile the two contrary statements; and they did not undertake to do so. They simply affirmed that both were equally true. The mystery of the concept could not be demonstrated to the intellect; but they refused to dismiss the structure of reality by leaving out either one or the other of the two truths that created the mystery.

It is important to keep in mind that Christianity is a monotheism no less inflexible than Judaism or Mohammedanism. Often there are present-day Christians who are in danger of forgetting this fact and slipping unconsciously in their thinking into Tri-theism, or the worship of three Gods. But it was to avoid this error and make unmistakably clear the fact of the oneness of God that the makers of the historic creeds of Christendom went to such painstaking lengths in formulating their doctrinal statements so as to leave no doubt about the matter. As an illustration of their concern at this point, take a few sentences from the Athanasian Creed, which in itself is a great series of reiterations of this basic truth:

For there is one person (persona) of the Father, another of the Son, and another of the Holy Ghost. But the Godhead of the Father, of the Son, and of the Holy Ghost is all one. The Father eternal, the Son eternal, and the Holy Ghost eternal; and yet there are not three Eternals, but one Eternal. Likewise the Father is almighty; the Son is almighty; and the Holy Ghost is almighty. And yet there are not three Almighties but one Almighty. So the Father is God, the Son is God, and the Holy Ghost is God; and yet there are not three Gods but one God, so that the Unity in Trinity and the Trinity in Unity is to be worshipped.

No one can imprison in a form of words the entire truth

of God. The doctrine of the Trinity was never intended to be taken as a literal description of reality; rather it should be regarded as a functional concept, a formula as it were, which can prove useful in helping us keep in mind the most important truths of God as men have come to know them in history and personal experience. Someone has said of the doctrine that while one may be in danger of losing his soul by denying it, he is in equal danger of losing his wits in trying to understand it. But it is not necessary to understand it, if by understanding it we mean the ability to visualize it. The formula can prove highly valuable to us even though we may never be able to form a mental image of it.

The Trinitarian concept is an example of what the Danish physicist Niels Bohr called "the theory of complementarity," which holds that there are certain physical entities which cannot be adequately described without using terms that are mutually contradictory of each other. For instance, physicists for several years past have held separate and contrary views of the nature of light, some regarding light as a wave and others as a particle, yet each view yielding definite results when put into effect. Is light made up of particles such as a stream of billiard balls, or is it a wave similar to a ripple of water? The answer is that it is neither one nor the other but both. In the same way, it would seem that the only approximately adequate conception we can form of a divine Being is under the form of a contradiction.

No one can visualize the multiform existence of God without falsifying it, for the more we attempt to do so the farther from the truth we find ourselves. But if we hold clearly and steadily in our minds the two realities which the Trinitarian formula embodies—the truths that God was fully present in Christ, and that he is one—we need not worry about the fact that we are unable to understand it or to make a mental image of it.

Since God is the awesome and impenetrable mystery in whom all meaning is conceived and whom no statement exhausts, any description of his being must necessarily be expressed in symbolic terms. Innumerable are the attempts of man to express in outward form or language the nature and reality of God. Primitive man has his idols, such as bulls or birds, snakes or beetles, or even images made in human form. It is not the idol itself that is worshipped, but the reality for which the idol stands. The Jews, for whom the making of images was an abomination, had a wealth of verbal symbolism with which they described the Divine attributes. They called the object of their worship Elohim, El Shaddi, "The mighty one of Jacob," "The Rock," "The Shepherd of Israel," "The Waters of Shiloah that go softly," "He that abideth of old." These were merely verbal descriptions of that which in itself was beyond all description.

The doctrine of the Trinity is the summation of all revealed wisdom and combines the essential truths of the Christian revelation in one august symbol. It is the truest and most comprehensive conceptualization of the being of God which the human mind has yet formulated. In it the Church confesses that the transcendent God—"the high and lofty One which inhabiteth eternity, whose name is Holy"—is not only the self-revealing God but is also the self-imparting God who has inspired prophets and apostles, nerved the martyr for his heroic gift of self, sustained the saint in his quest for holiness, and is still at work in the world, ready at all times to do more for each of us than we can ask or think. For this reason, Christians worship the one God, throned from everlasting to everlasting in the immutability of his three-fold image.

It is ever true that as one ascends into the loftier and purer forms of worship the symbolism becomes more refined and exalted. In a master stroke of poetic genius, Dante symbolizes the being of God by an indivisible atomic point. In the closing moments of his Beatific Vision, he is shown a single point of intensest light, so sharp no eye could bear up against its keenness and so small that the least star on earth would appear a moon beside it, yet he was told, "Heaven, and all nature, hangs upon that point." The poet then says:

In the deep clear substance of the sublime Light I beheld three circles of three colours and of one dimension; and the second appeared to be reflected from the first, as rainbow is from rainbow, and the third resembled fire proceeding equally from both.

Then, as his vision deepens, the great seer is made aware of the fact that the human Christ has carried man's nature into the very being of God; and he expresses this ultimate truth in a great apostrophe to the divine Trinity:

> O eternal Light
> Sole in Thyself that dwellest, and of Thyself
> Sole understood, past, present, or to come:
> Thou smilest, on that circling, which in Thee
> Seemed as reflected splendor, while I mused;
> For therein, methought, in its own hue
> Beheld our image painted.

The hard-core fact made evident by the resurrection and ascension of Christ is that at the heart of eternal reality there is someone whom we already know something about. The revelation of God's character and glory has been given us by One, who in his earthly life sweated in a carpenter's shop, watched the sunsets fade and walked among the lilies. In him the unknown has become known and knowable. He is now at the helm of things; and "unto his measures moveth the whole."

The vision which so fascinated the Apostle Paul in his Epistle to the Ephesians was the action of God in a great reconciling movement in which he sought to gather together all the scattered and disparate elements of creation into one master design. This age-long intention was accomplished in the death and resurrection of Christ, through whom a transcendent reservoir of power has been released in the world. The risen Christ has thus become a part of the structure of the thoughts and aspirations of men and the shaping influence of the cosmos. From his seat in the heavenlies—that invisible sphere of spiritual activity which constitutes the ruling forces of the universe—the power of the risen Christ is manifest and made available to the spiritual and eternal society called the Church, of which he is Head. Therefore the great Apostle prays for his Christian brethren that their eyes might be opened to the transcendent greatness of this power working on their behalf and says:

I never give up praying for you; and this is my prayer. That God, the God of our Lord Jesus Christ and the all-glorious Father, will give you spiritual wisdom and the insight to know more of him: that you may receive that inner illumination of the spirit which will make you realize how great is the hope to which he is calling you—the magnificence and splendor of the inheritance promised to Christians—and how tremendous is the power available to us who believe in God. That power is the same divine energy which was demonstrated in Christ when he raised him from the dead and gave him the place of supreme honor in Heaven—a place that is infinitely superior to any conceivable command, authority, power or control, and which carries with it a name far beyond any that could ever be used in this world or in the world to come. God has placed everything under the power of Christ and has set him up as head of everything for the Church. For the Church is his body, and in that body lives fully the one who fills the whole wide universe. (1:15-23)

CHAPTER SEVEN

THE CHRIST WHO IS TO COME

In an important address before Parliament a few years before his death, Sir Winston Churchill spoke of the human predicament and the threat of universal extinction now hanging over the race and said: "What ought we to do? Which way shall we turn to save our lives and the future of the world? It does not matter so much to old people. They are going soon anyway. But I find it poignant to look at youth in all its activities and ardor, and most of all to watch little children playing their merry games, and wonder what would lie before them if God wearied of mankind."

Mr. Churchill wondered if there could be a limit to God's willingness to carry on the human experiment. Is this a possibility? Will the divine patience ever wear out and God decide to junk his creation? The cynic could find discernible reasons for thinking this course might be justified. Mark Twain, whose humor could be quite acrid, said he sometimes got so fed up with people that he was almost sorry Noah hadn't missed the boat. The same viewpoint was given a slightly different turn by the more articulate Puritan who said, "I don't see how God can stand all the sin in the world; I can hardly stand it myself."

The issue Sir Winston raised as to the possibility of the human race exhausting the patience of God, and thus ultimately altering the divine strategy, is something quite foreign to our customary train of thought. We have pretty much taken the stability of the natural order for granted and assumed that things will continue indefinitely as they are. But this may not necessarily be the case. The Deism of the eighteenth century, which regarded physical nature as a closed system in which nothing exceptionable could ever happen, has given way to the more dynamic conception of a universe in which there can be upsets and surprises. Unpredictable events may now take place in the physical world, events which were previously regarded as never occurring within the framework of a more static mechanism.

In the early part of 1956, an astronomical prodigy took place in outer space that made the possibility of the human experiment being brought to an abrupt end through some catastrophic occurrence in nature something more than an academic matter. The sun blazed up in a sudden spectacular glory which made all massive and prodigious explosions of man fade into insignificance. With practically no advance warning and with the force of millions of hydrogen bombs, seething blazing gases on our star shot up in a solar flame 80,000 miles high. Within a matter of a few minutes, cosmic rays fifteen times more intense than any ever measured penetrated the earth's atmosphere and everything in it. The phenomenon of sun spots had been observed and studied by astronomers previously; but nothing on this scale had ever been known before. A slightly higher degree of radiation would have annihilated the human race in a matter of a few minutes.

Astronomers were surprised and baffled by the awesome event. This unusual activity in outer space should make us aware that ultimately our well-being, our very existence, is dependent upon forces and developments over which man has no control. It can be a healthy reminder of our creatureliness before the transcendent God who brought these awful and imponderable forces into being and by which he can say to the proud and puny man he has created, in the sobering words of Islam, "The heaven and the earth and all between, thinkest thou I made them *in jest?*"

Lesser, but recurring, flare-ups of the sun have taken place since the 1956 event, one of which caused momentary, though grave, concern for the safety of the Apollo 12 crew of astronauts during their flight to the moon. The frequency of these eruptions underscores the fact that universal extinction is no longer a theoretical matter but a distinct possibility that could take place at any time. A heavier stream of radioactive particles from the sun, a gigantic earthquake, an eruption of earth's central heat, or any number of unpredictable events in the physical world about us could easily bring an end to human life on this planet.

In addition to these dangers, there is the possibility of a man-made catastrophe. For the first time in history, man can destroy himself by the explosion of a super-hydrogen bomb of sufficient power to shatter the globe, by the pollution of his rivers and oceans by insecticides, by bacterial warfare, or in a number of other possible ways. President Kennedy warned that 100 million Americans would die in the first hour of a nuclear exchange. Following this horrendous event, there would be left an unliveable planet covered by the radioactive debris of human wreckage and universal contamination of the earth and atmosphere. It is clearly evident that history can end either by the action of physical forces beyond man's control, or by a nuclear holocaust set off by man himself. In either case, the end result is the same.

Modern astronomers have generally held the position that life on the earth will eventually come to an end. This view is based on the general principle of entropy, which holds that energy like water tends to run down hill, and that the sun like a rundown clock will finally reach a state of "heat-death," probably exploding as stars frequently do in the final stages of their deterioration. There is a striking similarity between this view of the end and that expressed in the Epistle of Second Peter: "The heavens shall pass away with a great noise, and the elements be dissolved with fervent heat, and the earth and the works therein shall be burnt up."(3:10)

The Biblical writers looked upon the end of human existence on the earth as being near at hand. Except for a small segment of millennarian thought, most moderns have thought of it as being in the distant future. What is new in the present situation is not the possibility of a last generation but the possibility that *ours* could be the last generation. It is no longer a theoretical matter that the curtain could be rung down upon human history either by some cosmic upset, or by a fatal act of defiance of the will of God on the part of man.

Eschatology—the doctrine of the last things—was a major concern of New Testament thought. The first Christians equated their belief in the end of the world with the second coming of Christ. Following Pentecost, apostolic preaching was impregnated with the idea. Men turned from the worship of idols to God to await for his Son from heaven. At his coming the consummation of history would take place. This return was felt to be so near at hand that some of the Thessalonian Christians quit their jobs in order to wait for the event to happen; and the Apostle Paul found it necessary to write a letter of correction to the church in order to clarify the situation. The poet, Frederic W. H. Myers expresses the fervor of the advent hope which animated the early Christian community:

> Hark what a sound, and too divine for hearing,
> Stirs on the earth and trembles in the air!
> Is it the thunder of the Lord's appearing?
> Is it the music of the people's prayer?
>
> Surely he cometh, and a thousand voices
> Call to the saints and to the deaf are dumb;
> Surely he cometh, and the earth rejoices
> Glad in his coming who hath sworn, I come.

Arnold Toynbee points out the distinctiveness of this belief of Christianity among world religions when he says, "There is one feature of the Christian mythology which seems to have no precedent; and that is the interpretation of the future coming of the Saviour or Messiah as the future return to earth of an historical figure who has already lived on the earth as a human being. In the concept of the Second

Coming the motif of Withdrawal-and-Return attains its deepest spiritual meaning."

How did the notion of the second coming originate? The strength and vitality of the idea in the early church suggests that the belief did not spring out of thin air but was based on a responsible source. In the nature of the case, the idea must have been rooted in actual statements of Jesus which the disciples on numerous occasions heard him make. That Jesus himself was responsible for the belief is evident in his so-called apocalyptic utterances and the teaching of many of his parables. Indeed this eschatological element in the New Testament is sufficient to cause a great biblical scholar such as Albert Schweitzer, even while holding that Jesus was mistaken in his eschatology, to base his entire concept of Jesus' person and mission upon it.

At his trial before the Sanhedrim, when asked by Caiaphas to tell them plainly whether or not he was the Jewish Messiah, the narrative relates that Jesus replied in the affirmative and then added the startling assertion, "And ye shall see the Son of Man sitting on the right hand of power and coming in the clouds of heaven." (Mk. 14:62) Once as he and his disciples were leaving Herod's Temple in Jerusalem and a member of the group called attention to its goodly stones and massive architecture, Jesus is recorded as saying that the time was coming when it would all be torn down and not one stone left standing upon another. A little later, some of his disciples asked him privately to tell them when the event he referred to would take place and what were "the signs of thy coming and the end of the world." In a vivid discourse Jesus describes the future desolations that actually occurred a generation later when the Roman army under Titus destroyed Jerusalem in 70 A.D. and razed the temple to the ground. He then went on to declare, "Then shall they see the Son of Man coming in the clouds of heaven with power and great glory." (Mk. 13:26)

Many of his parables, such as the Ten Virgins, the Talents, and the Faithful Steward, which were told to illustrate truths of the approaching kingdom, are built around the concept of a withdrawal and return of the Lord of the story. Frequently they end with an injunction to watchfulness: "Watch ye, for ye know not the day nor hour when the Son of Man cometh." One of the most dramatic and colorful of them all—the parable of the Sheep and Goats—carries the imagery of a Great Assize which will take place at the end of history following this return: "When the Son of Man shall come in his glory and all the holy angels with him, then shall he sit upon the throne of his glory and before him shall be gathered all nations and he shall separate them one from another as a shepherd separates his sheep from his goats."(Mt. 25:31)

Except for certain of the smaller sects whose preaching is almost totally eschatological, the doctrine of the second coming has received scant attention from the contemporary pulpit. Yet the idea is too deeply embedded in the teaching of Jesus and the thought of the early church to be lightly set aside. To be sure, such descriptions as the above are semi-poetic or symbolic images which cannot be taken in a strictly literal fashion, as has been done too often in the past; but this is not to say that we are at liberty to disregard the hard-core truth they embody. Nothing Jesus ever said is without significance; and while we need not take all his sayings literally, we are obligated to take them all seriously.

In present-day theological circles, there are two general interpretations of the nature of the event. The first of these, which is known as "realized eschatology," maintains that the second coming of Christ has already occurred, or is in the process of taking place. The argument for this view is based on the idea of the Paraclete in John's Gospel and interprets the Greek word *parousia* to mean not so much a future coming as an abiding reality. It is a form of metaphysical gradualism which stresses the present reality and dynamic of the kingdom and holds that even though well-nigh invisible the kingdom of God is present and at work in the world.

The second interpretation is that something absolutely special is going to take place at the end of history which will be evident to all the world when it happens. According to this view, the kingdom will not attain its final completion without the overt intervention of God in a cataclysmic event of unprecedented dimensions. The distinction between the two interpretations has to do with the nature of judgment. The first regards judgment as something present and continuous and as the inevitable will of righteousness working itself out in the processes of history; while the second thinks of it as the finality and decisiveness of a universal denouement at which the kingdom of God will be fully revealed and history consummated.

The concept of a return of Christ has been the occasion of much misunderstanding, futile speculation, and gross distortion. Its chronology has been a persistent source of confusion from the beginning. The early church was uncertain as to when the event would take place. In his discourses on the destruction of Jerusalem, Jesus is recorded to have said, "This generation shall not pass away till all these things shall be fulfilled." (Lk. 21:32) The disciples seemed to have been confused at the time as to the exact meaning of the words. Whether in his statement Jesus was referring to the destruction of Jerusalem, which seems to have been his likely meaning, or whether he was speaking of the end of the world was not clear.

This uncertainty concerning the future timing of the event has continued down to the present day. There has scarcely been a period since the first century when spokesmen were not predicting an early return of the Lord, particularly during periods of crises and stress such as the Saracen invasion of Europe in the eighth century, the Protestant Reformation, the French and American Revolutions, and the two World Wars. During the Hussite Wars the Bohemians expected the *parousia* to occur immediately. Millitz of Kromeriz, a precursor of John Huss, set the date between 1365 and 1367. The Anabaptists thought it would take place in connection with the Peasants' War of 1525. There have been innumerable instances of such date-setting since that time, all of them disappointing and many of them having unfortunate results.

A single example of the unfortunate results of date-setting is that of William Miller, a Baptist preacher of Low Hampton, New York, and founder of the modern adventist sects. Miller took figures from Daniel and the Book of Revelation and proved in five different ways that the world would come to an end on March 15, 1843. His announcement caused great excitement. Many of his followers sold or gave away their property, bought white ascension robes, and spent the night of March 14th in rapt anticipation. Some of them climbed on haystacks or barn roofs to get a better view of the happenings that were scheduled to occur. When the sun rose many of them were disappointed that nothing took place; others were greatly relieved. Miller himself was much let down that his prophesy did not pan out. He re-examined his figures and charts and set a new date for 1844. Again he was to be disappointed. He did not live long after this but died a broken old man.

Similar regrettable fiascoes have taken place literally hundreds of times in the past. A vigorous sect has flourished in recent years on the slogan, "Millions now living will never die." From pulpit and mass media, contemporary evangelists, whose zeal often outruns their knowledge, preach an imminent return of Christ with vehemence and with the certainty of first-hand knowledge as to its approximate date. All of this in spite of the fact that Jesus himself disclaimed any knowledge of its timing. When the specific question was asked by his disciples he is on record as having told them, "Of that day and hour knoweth no man, no, not the angels which are in heaven, neither the Son, but my Father only." (Mk. 13:32) If the Lord of Glory himself left indefinite the date of his return, it seems reasonable to assume that his followers could hardly be more specific about it than he was.

A more serious distortion of the idea of the second coming has been the misunderstanding of its essential nature. The event has frequently been pictured as a universal display of divine wrath such as would suggest that God's mercy at the end of time has been finally and irrevocably terminated. According to this type of preaching, the redeeming God of Bethlehem and Calvary will then become the destroying God who will not only obliterate sin but the sinner as well. Never again will there be joy in heaven over one sinner that repents, because repentance is no longer acceptable. From henceforth the *modus operandi* of divine mercy will be altered because God has either reached the end of his patience or the limits of his power. But this is to distort the very gospel such persons have been called to proclaim. A touching reminder of this truth took place during the flight to the moon of Apollo 8.

In some respects the most remarkable thing about the flight of astronauts Borman, Lovell and Anders on Christmas 1968 was not the closer view of the moon but the more distanced view of the earth. The Russian cosmonaut Gagarin, had caught a glimpse of the curvature of the earth as he circled it on April 11, 1961, at a height of 180 miles; but the three astronauts saw it for the first time from a distance of 240,000 miles away. With their own eyes they beheld the world "whole and round and beautiful and small" suspended in empty space. Jim Lovell, in describing the scene from the capsule, stated that they could see no colors but black and white throughout the universe except back on the earth. "There we could see the royal blue of the seas, the tans and browns of the land, and the white of the clouds. It was just another body, really, about four times bigger than the moon. But it held all the hope and all the life and all the things that the crew of Apollo 8 knew and loved. It was the most beautiful thing there was to see in all the heavens."

Among the millions of television viewers who heard the astronauts give this description, there was at least one who found himself pondering afresh the ancient mystery expressed in that amazing statement from the heart of the Christian religion: "For God so loved the world that he gave his only begotten Son." This little lonely planet of ours, floating in the depths of infinite space, has been a special object of divine concern. God loved it once—will he become tired of it? It would be a simple matter for him to blot out his creation if he wants to. But does he want to? There are those whose preaching would suggest that he does. In fact, such persons often sound as though they thought he would take real pleasure in doing it—at least they themselves would under the circumstances.

But if Christianity is true, it seems that God is not interested in destroying the world. He is trying to save it. The God whom the poet Edward Markham describes as "the One forever hurling back the curse" and who unceasingly tramps the universe to seek and to save that which is lost is not likely to give the thing up as a bad job. In Jesus Christ we see not just a man whom men call Saviour but the eternal God who means to save, no matter to what lengths he may have to go.

"The world in which we live," said the advisory commission on the main theme of the Second Assembly of the World Council of Churches, "is the world that God has loved from all eternity in Jesus Christ. To this world God has spoken through Him. . . . Our hope is not the projection of our desires upon an unknown future, but the product in us of God's acts in history, and above all of His act in raising Jesus Christ from the dead. That mighty event is faith's assurance that Christ has overcome the world and all the powers of evil, sin, and death; it is the beginning of a new life in the power of the Spirit; it is the guarantee of God's promise that in His good time His victory will be manifest to all, His Kingdom come in glory, and He Himself be known everywhere as King."

The doctrine of the second coming carries two important implications: first, that the ultimate purpose of God for man lies beyond history; and second, that the clew to this purpose is revealed in Christ.

The first of these ideas is rooted in the New Testament concept of the kingdom of God as being both *in* time and *beyond* time. In a true and real sense Jesus regarded the kingdom as already established upon the earth—"the kingdom of God is at hand," it is a present reality. At the same time he spoke of it in its eschatalogical sense as something yet to come. Both of these aspects are embodied in the Lord's Prayer in which we are enjoined to pray: "Thy kingdom *come*," while at the same time we recognize that "Thine *is* the kingdom, and the power, and the glory."

The New Testament nowhere guarantees that human existence will ever reach a stage of perfection on this plane of life; and although we hope it will, Christianity would not be disturbed if it should not. The Christian cannot abandon history as the sphere of God's activity and power; yet he is not dismayed when the historic process leads not to triumph but seeming defeat, for he looks for a consummation beyond history. Another war may come in which millions will die before their time and the planet itself will be left in ashes; but this will not stop the processes of God or destroy his ultimate purpose for mankind. God is redeeming the world in terms of eternity; and time does not count, only values count.

If the world should come to an end, the essential things of the Christian faith are not changed in the least. A Christian's well-being is not conditioned on his physical survival, or even the survival of the globe itself. Human existence has always been built on the edge of a precipice; and the end of the world does not alter the permanent human situation, or change the fact of eventual death. As the Scotchman described it, "Life is a risky business and very few of us get out of the world alive." A hundred percent of us will die, regardless of whether we are all wiped out together in a world holocaust or each one of us dies naturally one at a time.

If man will cooperate with God in the social melee, the world may yet be fair; but if he should fail to do so on the earthly level, the possibilities are still not exhausted. We are taught to work and pray for the coming of the kingdom. This a Christian must do; for it is ever true that if we do not attempt the impossible, even the possible cannot be realized. But even if all the wider social issues of the world were settled—war banished from the earth, poverty eliminated, and all racial discrimination and injustice removed—there would still be vast and far-reaching needs of man unmet. Grace cannot come from gadgets, as J. B. Priestley reminds us. "The dishes in the bakelite houses of the future may not break, but the heart can; even a man with six bathrooms may find life flat, stale, and unprofitable."

Christianity's grasp of cosmic values relegates material values such as food and health, clothing and shelter to their true dimensional significance. God has been ever more concerned to make men holy than to make them comfortable; and the high significance of human life does not lie in the mechanism of its social institutions, but in the fact that human personality is being forged in the crucible of the world's workshop into something that has meaning in a wider sphere of existence. The world is the preparation for an ultimate reality; and there are indications that big things are ahead.

The second corollary of the advent doctrine is that the clew to God's purpose for man is revealed in Christ. The World Council of Churches in its meeting at Evanston expressed this truth when it declared, "The glory of God, once manifested in Jesus Christ to those who had eyes to see, will be revealed to the whole created universe. . . . As judge of the world He will appear as God's final revelation to every ear and every eye and as the final goal of all God's ways."

The Christian belief is that the second coming of Christ will be a great breaking open of things—a universal disclosure of divine realities. Things that heretofore have lain hidden, or only dimly apprehended by the masses of mankind, will be made clear to everyone, so that even the unthinking or spiritually obtuse cannot fail to see them. At that time Christ will be unmistakably revealed as the embodiment of the Divine Intention and as the inevitable pattern of every life. The culmination of history may therefore be looked upon as an infinite *Ecce Homo* in which every eye shall see the glory of God in the face of Jesus Christ and every tongue shall exclaim, "Behold the Man!" Confronted by the truth and grace of the "First born of all Creation," the universal conscience will instinctively declare, "This, under God, I was created to become!"

Christianity is saturated with the idea that man is set apart for an inconceivably high destiny yet to be realized. Since the advent of modern science, this destiny has often been pictured in terms of man's control over his physical environment. In one of his literary productions, H. G. Wells describes the man of the future as the master technician who, after he has attained complete mastery of the physical universe, will then "reach out his hands amid the stars and laugh." But the problem goes beyond that of technological manipulation.

Man's chief concern at the present is to dominate the material universe; but the far more pressing matter is that he learn to dominate himself. Increasing knowledge of scientific techniques creates super-difficulties but not super-men. It is an awful thing to know what God knows and not want what he wants for us. Persons who travel to the moon or other distant places change their positions in space but do not thereby change their essential characters. They find that however far they may travel into space they carry themselves along, with the same prejudices, self-will, pride, and selfishness that they had when they set out. The big problem, therefore, is not the conquest of physical nature but the conquest of the human spirit.

The task of mastering the skills of technology is relatively simple compared to that of transforming individuals into responsible, trustworthy creatures who always do the right and who can be trusted to use their God-given powers unselfishly for the common good. Lord Acton's dictum that power corrupts and absolute power corrupts absolutely had its one exception. The spiritually Perfect Man, with transcendent power at his disposal, never used this power for his personal advantage. He was willing to multiply the loaves and fishes to feed the hungry multitude; but he would not turn stones into bread to satisfy his own hunger.

A spiritually immature individual today who suddenly found himself possessed of similar miraculous powers as those possessed by Jesus would probably open a restaurant before nightfall. At least this, in principle, is what collective man is now doing. With ample means at our disposal to feed the hungry of the world, America's national policy has been to restrict production in order to keep prices up; and while the rest of the world goes hungry—as well as one-fifth of our own population—to squander our national resources on trips to the moon and the fabulous costs of futile military outlays.

It would seem that the end design of creation is the realization of a morally superior order of beings—men of great hearts as well as great intellects, completely liberated from the human passions of egotism, greed, and lust for power, men to whom the keys of universal nature may be safely entrusted. In fact, this is what Christianity is all about. "In the New Testament," says the late Principal L. P. Jacks in *The Lost Radiance of the Christian Religion*, "we are introduced to a conception of man which represents him as a vast reservoir of spiritual force, unused, undeveloped, perhaps even unborn, waiting for liberation, and destined when liberated to clothe him with splendid virtues, to expand his being over an enormous range, to make his garments whiter than any fuller on earth can white them, and his countenance to shine as the sun."

The clear intent of all this is that the human creature is designed to take on qualities of the Divine. Oh, we're sunk enough, God knows it! But it is hardly likely that Jesus would have taught us to call God, Father, if he had not thought there was something about us that is akin to God. The motif of the New Testament is expressed in a single sentence from the opening chapter of the Fourth Gospel: "As many as received him to them gave he *power to become the sons of God.*" In the great eighth chapter of Romans, the Apostle Paul speaks of this age-long intention and says, "Whom he did foreknow, he also did predestinate to be conformed to the image (*eikon*, or likeness) of his Son, that

174

he might be the firstborn among many brethren."

Christianity is clear and unanimous that the final purpose of God is the achievement of a spirit world, peopled by human personalities who have taken on the moral qualities of the Elder Brother. In other words—though it sounds almost irreverent to say so—it seems that God's far-reaching intention for mankind is that we should all become *little Christs.* It was this end the Elder of Ephesus had in mind when he exclaims, "Behold, how great is the love that the Father has shown to us! Now are we the sons of God, and it does not yet appear what we shall be; but we know that when he shall appear, we shall be like him, for we shall see him as he is." (I John 3:1)

This new vision of God's high purpose for man is the source of the joy that throbs through the early Christian literature which Dean Church regarded as the most solemn thing in history. It is plain that we are cut out for great things. "Whatever we may have to go through now," says Paul, "is less than nothing compared with the magnificent future God has planned for us. The whole creation is on tiptoe to see the wonderful sight of the sons of God coming into their own. The world of creation cannot as yet see reality, not because it chooses to be blind, but because in God's purpose it has been so limited—yet it has been given hope. And the hope is that in the end the whole of created life will be rescued from the tyranny of change and decay, and have its share in that magnificent liberty which can only belong to the children of God." (Romans 8:18-21) The poet Tennyson, with penetrating beauty, expresses the idea of this cosmic goal in the closing canto of his *In Memoriam* when he speaks of

> One God, one law, one element,
> And one far-off divine event
> To which the whole creation moves.

When the Apostle Paul describes the Big Event that lies

ahead as "The Unveiling of the Sons of God," he seems to be thinking of a distant time at the culmination of the ages when, as a grand climax to all things, universal nature will display its finished product in a kind of spectacular and infinite dress-parade. The curtain will then be lifted upon a vast assembly of human spirits that have reached the highest order of spiritual attainment, a host of reverent and obedient sons, drawn together from all parts of the universe and united under the banner of the Social Christ.

The culmination of this massive goal—sometimes spoken of in the New Testament as "the mystery of the will of God"—is the realization of an eternal order of faith, *a grand family of holy spirits.* When man has gone through his various stages of rootings and groundings and has sloughed off his egotisms and his hypocrisies, his greed and his selfishness, and has become a completely selfless creature dedicated to the service of others, then he can be given transcendent powers heretofore reserved to God alone. Those who have been faithful over a few things can be made rulers over many things. A humble English Christian summed up the idea in a sentence which was written on the fly-leaf of his Bible and discovered shortly after his death: "We labor on till evening and for a reward God gives us the freedom of the universe."

This Grand Design has been God's intention from the beginning; but there is a perverse and stubborn element inherent in things which defies this intention. The Greeks called this something *hyle*—the intractable matter which is passively hostile to Psyche. This perverse and obdurate quality in human nature inhibits the creative end and resists any moral advance. God would give man the best but man does not always want the best. The divine purpose is that man should become Godlike; but to attain this end, something was necessary to overcome man's reluctance and secure his cooperation. Some catalytic agent, vast and compelling, was needful to effect a spiritual breakthrough and accomplish the cosmic forward push.

Christianity holds that the death of Christ was the Divine

Catalyst that made a qualitative difference in the evolution of the race. The Great Sacrifice was the thing by which God touched the world, and brought "many sons unto glory." Scripture will not let us forget that the remaking of man has been a costly undertaking. In the closing scene of the Bible, an uncountable multitude which has attained unto cosmic dignity and status is described as singing an unending gloria "to him that loved us and loosed us from our sins in his own blood, and hath made us kings and priests unto his God and his Father." The mystery of Divine compassion is the basis of man's hope. At the heart of the Christian religion is the sense of an Infinite Obligation that can never be repaid, only recognized and accepted with unspeakable gratitude. This is the great matter that neither time nor philosophy can change.

Harnack, the late German theologian, says that Christianity gives us two things—a goal and power to move toward the goal. The goal itself is clear. "To become like Jesus Christ," says Henry Drummond, "is the only thing in the world worth caring for, the thing before which every ambition of man is folly and all lower achievement vain." This is the ideal that beckons the soul. But something more than the ideal is necessary. We need help to attain unto the ideal. Christ is not only the goal of human existence, he is the One from whom we receive power to move toward the goal.

Earth's divine Guest has come and gone. His visit represents the central fact of the human story. The memory of it will remain as mankind's glimpse of what God is and what man was created to become. But memory is not enough. We live by what is alive and real for us at the present. The memory of a death is simply the memory of a death; but a resurrection is an altogether different matter, and means that the person who died continues to live. What we celebrate at Easter is no inert fact "stranded on the shores of the oblivious years"; rather, it is the present living power of One who superseded death and is awaiting each of us in the invisible realm of the spirit.

To talk this way may sound quite tenuous and unreal for

many who read these words. A regrettable number of people have picked flowers from life's garden without ever meeting the Gardener himself. But there are countless others for whom Christ is more real than husband or wife, parents or children, and who confidently look forward to a life with him in the unending future. His final promise, given on the eve of his crucifixion as he himself looked across the chasm of death, was: "I go to prepare a place for you that where I am there ye shall be also." Critics may explain these words away if they will—for many of them, explaining things away is their stock in trade—but the promise still stands. There is a reality that the world overlooks, which for some of us is the most precious fact on earth.

We and God have business with each other; and it is not likely that anything will ever change this permanent situation. The world may pass away but he that doeth the will of God abideth forever. There are certain great Indestructibles that wars do not wipe out nor death obliterates. Even though the moon may become littered with the debris of earth, the sun grow dim, and the stars fade out, the eternal purpose of God in Christ remains fixed. The Cross will continue to tower over the wrecks of time, commerce with the Infinite will still go on, and that One Face will never vanish.

Someone has defined Christianity as mysticism centered in Christ. The crux of the matter is a personal relationship between the believer and his Lord so vital that nothing else in all the world can matter much and all aspirations of the heart and decisions of the will spring from that fulcrum. Frederic W. H. Myers' *Saint Paul*—a poem of some hundred and fifty stanzas that has been described as the best interpretation of the soul of Paul outside the New Testament—illustrates this fact. Its opening stanza is a meditative brooding in which the great Apostle seems to be talking to himself as much as to others:

Christ! I am Christ's! and let the name suffice you,
Ay, for me too He greatly hath sufficed:

> Lo with no winning words I would entice you,
> Paul has no honour and no friend but Christ.

The closing stanza of the poem embodies the very essence of Christian mysticism as Paul asserts the all-sufficiency and finality of Christ:

> Yea thro' life, death, thro' sorrow and thro' sinning
> He shall suffice me, for he hath sufficed:
> Christ is the end, for Christ was the beginning,
> Christ the beginning, for the end is Christ.

As a student in college, the writer has an inspired memory of hearing for the first time the noted lecturer, author, and internationally known Christian spokesman, Dr. Sherwood Eddy, relate a memorable experience of the power of Christ in his own life which took place at the turn of the century while he was serving as the Y.M.C.A. secretary for All-Asia. He told how, after graduating from Yale, he had gone to India with high hopes and enthusiasm; but within a year, he had broken down with overwork and was on the verge of nervous prostration. There had been overwork but not overflow. He had failed in his outward service because he had failed in his inward life.

Things finally reached the inevitable impasse. One night, unable to sleep, and too exhausted to get up, he cried to God to show him the way out. Of a sudden, and with the objectivity of a spoken word, the words of Jesus to the woman at the well came to hime: "Whosoever drinketh of this water shall thirst again; but whosoever drinketh of the water that I shall give him shall never thirst; but the water that I shall give him, shall be in him, a well of water springing up unto everlasting life." Eddy took these words as personally directed to himself and in desperation accepted the gift of life offered to him.

"I cannot explain it," said Eddy, "but I arose the next morning with a new faith. I had been exhausted, now I felt power surging through me. I had been depressed and defeated, now I knew triumph. On that day in November 1897 I began to drink of the innermost central Fountain of Life. God knows how many mistakes I have made since then; how many failures, how many faults and sins mar my record; but from that moment to the present, I have never known an hour of darkness, or despair, or even of discouragement. I mean this literally. For the past twenty-seven years Christ has been sufficient for all my needs; and I am certain that twenty-seven years from now, or twenty-seven thousand years from now, he will still be sufficient."

Eddy's electric words beat into my mind with peremptory insistence as I left the auditorium that night. "Twenty-seven years . . . twenty-seven thousand years from now Christ will be sufficient." Eventually I came to understand that drinking the water of life which Jesus promised (the life of God in the soul of man shared with his fellow men) was not confined to the single act of conversion but is a continuous process. The words do not mean "whosoever drinketh once shall never thirst again," as has often been erroneously interpreted; but in the original Greek they are in the present tense and mean "whosoever drinks and keeps on drinking" shall know the inflow and outflow of an abundant life. Years later, Eddy and I were thrown together in a close association that continued intermittently until his death. On one occasion, I reminded him of the testimony I had first heard him give and asked him if it still held good. His answer, expressed in a verse of Scripture, was instantaneous and unequivocal: "Jesus Christ the same yesterday and today and forever!"

To my late friend's testimony, I would add my personal witness to the finality and sufficiency of Christ for my own life. I dare not do less. From earliest childhood, when I first met him in the pages of the New Testament, I have felt his moral beauty and excellence. As I grew from boyhood to manhood and eventually became a minister of his gospel, his words became increasingly meaningful to me. His personal image, derived from the written records of his life, has

across the years and confronted
 in the sunset. Fellowship with
 of my life.

my service has been nothing to
fully inadequate and has been
 excess of selfishness, pride, and
 all, Christ has been the central
worship and the focus of all the
have fallen below his purpose for
creant to his will, in him I have
have denied him; and like Peter, I
 the compelling power of his

rivileged to know something that
—the immeasurable and transcen-
rgiven. In those realms of light
nd presence of the Eternal Christ
se who love and serve him, I look
broader and more effective service
im who loved me and gave himself
ity I shall belong to him. This, I
 on earth.

s of ruin untold,
f Thy sheltering fold,
s face to behold,
    Jesus I come to Thee.